Beyoncé
The Reign of Queen Bey

By Vanessa Oswald

Portions of this book originally appeared in
Beyoncé by Cherese Cartlidge.

LUCENT
P R E S S

Published in 2020 by
Lucent Press, an Imprint of Greenhaven Publishing, LLC
353 3rd Avenue
Suite 255
New York, NY 10010

Designer: Deanna Paternostro
Editor: Vanessa Oswald

Library of Congress Cataloging-in-Publication Data

Names: Oswald, Vanessa, author.
Title: Beyoncé: the reign of Queen Bey / Vanessa Oswald.
Description: New York : Lucent Press, 2020. | Series: People in the news |
  Includes bibliographical references and index.
Identifiers: LCCN 2018043703 (print) | LCCN 2018044121 (ebook) | ISBN
  9781534567726 (eBook) | ISBN 9781534567719 (pbk. book) | ISBN
  9781534567061 (library bound book)
Subjects: LCSH: Beyoncé, 1981- —Juvenile literature. | Singers—United
  States—Biography—Juvenile literature.
Classification: LCC ML3930.K66 (ebook) | LCC ML3930.K66 O78 2020 (print) |
  DDC 782.42164092 [B]—dc23
LC record available at https://lccn.loc.gov/2018043703

Printed in the United States of America

CPSIA compliance information: Batch #BS19KL: For further information contact Greenhaven Publishing LLC, New York,
New York, at 1-844-317-7404.

Please visit our website, www.greenhavenpublishing.com. For a free color
catalog of all our high-quality books, call toll free 1-844-317-7404 or fax
1-844-317-7405.

Contents

Foreword

We live in a world where the latest news is always available and where it seems we have unlimited access to the lives of the people in the news. Entire television networks are devoted to news about politics, sports, and entertainment. Social media has allowed people to have an unprecedented level of interaction with celebrities. We have more information at our fingertips than ever before. However, how much do we really know about the people we see on television news programs, social media feeds, and magazine covers?

Despite the constant stream of news, the full stories behind the lives of some of the world's most newsworthy men and women are often unknown. Who was Gal Gadot before she became Wonder Woman? What does LeBron James do when he is not playing basketball? What inspires Lin-Manuel Miranda?

This series aims to answer questions like these about some of the biggest names in pop culture, sports, politics, and technology. While the subjects of this series come from all walks of life and areas of expertise, they share a common magnetism that has made them all captivating figures in the public eye. They have shaped the world in some unique way, and—in many cases—they are poised to continue to shape the world for many years to come.

These biographies are not just a collection of basic facts. They tell compelling stories that show how each figure grew to become a powerful public personality. Each book aims to paint a complete, realistic picture of its subject—from the challenges they overcame to the controversies they caused. In doing so, each book reinforces the idea that even the most famous faces on the news are real people who are much more complex than we are often shown in brief video clips or sound bites. Readers are also reminded that there is even more to a person than what they present to the world through social media posts, press releases, and interviews. The whole story of a person's life can only be discovered by digging beneath the surface of their public persona, and that is what this series allows readers to do.

The books in this series are filled with enlightening quotes from speeches and interviews given by the subjects, as well as quotes and anecdotes from those who know their story best: family, friends, coaches, and colleagues. All quotes are noted to provide guidance for further research. Detailed lists of additional resources are also included, as are timelines, indexes, and unique photographs. These text features come together to enhance the reading experience and encourage readers to dive deeper into the stories of these influential men and women.

Fame can be fleeting, but the subjects featured in this series have real staying power. They have fundamentally impacted their respective fields and have achieved great success through hard work and true talent. They are men and women defined by their accomplishments, and they are often seen as role models for the next generation. They have left their mark on the world in a major way, and their stories are meant to inspire readers to leave their mark, too.

Introduction

The Fate
of a True Superstar

As soon as young Beyoncé Knowles found music, she began influencing the people around her. Now known as Beyoncé Knowles-Carter or simply "Beyoncé," she has become a pop culture sensation, a role model for girls and young women, an inspiration for aspiring performers, and an advocate for several worthy causes. Thus far, she has reached numerous milestones in her life, but the night of January 20, 2009, stands out as especially significant. On that day, Barack Obama had been sworn in as president of the United States, becoming the nation's first African American president. The nation celebrated this historic event with 10 official inaugural balls in Washington, D.C. Barack and his wife Michelle Obama had asked Beyoncé to sing the opening song at the first of these inaugural balls. She proudly sang the Etta James classic "At Last," which she had recorded for the 2008 film *Cadillac Records*. One of the greatest honors of Beyoncé's career occurred that night as she sang for the new president and his wife during their first inaugural dance.

It was a memorable moment for Beyoncé, the Obamas, and the nation as well. As she sang, the Obamas danced nearby, smiling and speaking quietly to one another as they gracefully moved together around the dance floor. Beyoncé was wiping away tears by the end of the song and blew a kiss to them when she finished singing.

President Barack Obama danced with First Lady Michelle Obama as Beyoncé sang Etta James's "At Last" at his first inaugural ball.

When Beyoncé was asked to sing at the inaugural ball, she called the invitation "a dream come true." She added, "I could not be more honored and excited that they have asked me to be part of this moment in history."[1] Not only was it a huge honor for her to be asked to perform, but she had also worked hard to help Obama get elected. When Obama was campaigning for the presidency, Beyoncé traveled around the country with her husband, JAY-Z, to help promote the campaign. In addition, she postponed a concert in Japan in order to be in the United States on Election Day in November 2008.

For the 27-year-old Beyoncé Knowles-Carter, singing at the inaugural ball was a high point in an already impressive career. From her early days singing and dancing with what would become one of the best-selling female groups of all time, Destiny's Child, she had evolved into a songwriter, record producer, actress, model, and fashion designer. Today, she is recognized as one of the most iconic artists ever. She has been nominated for 66 Grammy Awards and has won more than 20. The woman known to millions of fans around the world as "Queen Bey" was destined for success from a very young age, given her talent, dedication, and the help, encouragement, and support of her parents.

Becoming a Superstar

Much of Beyoncé's success is due to her parents' help and influence. Both were deeply involved in her early career. Her mother's skills as a hairstylist and clothing designer, as well as her father's background as a top salesman, helped turn Beyoncé into a worldwide superstar. Her father used his business skills to help manage and promote her and Destiny's Child, while her mother used her hairstyling and designing skills to create a variety of classic looks for the girl group.

In addition, Beyoncé was professionally trained from a young age. She took dance classes, sang in the church choir, attended special magnet music schools, and participated in talent contests. She trained and worked hard to develop her singing voice, which is famous for its operatic range. As a child, she took vocal lessons with David Brewer, an operatic tenor. All of these experiences helped to hone her skills as a singer and performer and to build the confidence needed to appear onstage before huge crowds.

Beyoncé also seems to have inherited her parents' business expertise. Today, she is an entrepreneur in her own right. "I grew up watching my mom and dad work their butts off—and I learned a lot from them," Beyoncé said. "No matter what happened, they never quit."[2] This dedication has helped transform her into an entertainment superstar and successful businesswoman.

Beyoncé's Influence on the World

Beyoncé has become a role model for girls and young women of all races. While she has often demonstrated traditional Christian values and polite manners, she is also progressive in her outspokenness as a feminist and supporter of racial equality. She cherishes her family and close friends, and she tries to keep as much of her personal time with them out of the tabloids as she can.

Despite the wholesome side of her image seen offstage, Beyoncé's onstage persona is very different. For example, in person, her speaking voice is soft-spoken, with a gentle southern drawl. However, onstage she becomes a spitfire, belting out songs with a powerful, throaty voice. Contradictions such as this have helped generate public interest in this private-yet-extravagant entertainer.

Beyoncé makes an effort to balance her professional life and her private life, and she believes that what really matters is remaining kindhearted toward others. "What's important to me is me remaining the same person," she says, "me still treating people the same way, and me maintaining my personal relationship with God."[3] Beyoncé has managed to remain true to herself and to her loved ones after more than 20 years in show business. Despite

While Beyoncé has tried many things, singing is still her main passion.

running into a few controversies over the years, she has a positive mindset and is determined to push forward to new heights in her career. As she assumes various roles, such as talented performer, savvy businesswoman, and dedicated mother, she continues to reinvent herself over and over and intrigue her legions of fans every step of the way.

Chapter One

A Star in the Making

Some people are born to be entertainers. When they take their position on stage and the bright lights shine down, the crowd goes wild and is instantly captivated, unable to contain their excitement and eagerly anticipating all that is to follow. These performers never fail to bring together large crowds of loyal fans, and they have a massive influence on pop culture and the world as a whole. Beyoncé Knowles-Carter is one of these entertainers.

Born on September 4, 1981, Beyoncé Giselle Knowles grew up in Houston, Texas. She is the daughter of Mathew Knowles and Célestine Knowles Lawson (most commonly referred to as Tina), who met at a party in Houston and married a few years later, in 1980. When Beyoncé was five years old, the Knowles family welcomed another daughter, whom they named Solange. Despite their age difference, Beyoncé and Solange got along well as children and continue to be close as adults.

Tina was the driving force behind Beyoncé's unique name. It comes from Tina's maiden name, Beyincé. At first, Tina's parents were surprised by the choice; they worried Beyoncé would later resent it because it sounded like a last name. However, Tina stuck by her choice, believing that most people would not mistake the name Beyoncé for a surname. Beyoncé's father picked her middle name, Giselle.

Beyoncé's family heritage is every bit as unique as her name. Her father is African American, and her mother's side of the family has a varied ethnicity. Tina's mother, Agnéz Deréon, grew up in Louisiana. Agnés's ancestors were African American, Choctaw (American Indian), Haitian, and Louisiana Creole (descendants of European settlers). Tina's father, Lumis Beyincé, also from Louisiana, had ancestors who were French, Spanish, Chinese, and Indonesian.

Hardworking Role Models

Tina and Mathew Knowles both put their children first and were strong role models for them. Mathew worked as a salesman when the children were young. In the years before Beyoncé was born, he sold a variety of things, including telephone equipment. postage meters, and photocopiers. He also sold medical equipment such as CT scanners and MRI machines for Pickering International Medical Supplies. He began working for the Xerox Corporation a year or two before Beyoncé was born and was named salesman of the year three years in a row. Mathew worked for Xerox throughout the 1980s and part of the 1990s, earning a high salary. His example of hard work and success was an important influence on Beyoncé when she was a child.

Beyoncé had many role models growing up, including Whitney Houston, Michael Jackson, Janet Jackson, Madonna, Diana Ross, and Aretha Franklin. However, her greatest role model was her mother, Tina, who was also hardworking. She saved enough money from her part-time job as a hairstylist to open her own hair salon, which she called Headliners Hair Salon. The 24-chair salon was one of the largest—and most profitable—hair salons in Houston. As the owner and operator of Headliners, Tina would work long hours, but she still found time for her family and friends. She took her daughters to church every week, drove them to dance classes and recitals, cooked meals for the family, and made prom and wedding dresses for friends and family.

Tina taught her daughters the principle of hard work, something they both value. Beyoncé said, "Tina Knowles was my first example of what a powerful woman is. She shaped my thinking

Although Beyoncé's parents divorced when she was an adult, her family was close while she was growing up.

not so much by what she said, but what she did. At her salon she worked 13-hour days, managed her staff, styled hair, and gave out free advice to her clients. ... She worked hard for her family and never complained."[4]

Beyoncé worked at the salon as a young child, sweeping up hair from the floor for tips, which she saved to buy a season pass to Six Flags Over Texas, part of the Six Flags chain of amusement parks. She enjoyed being in the salon so much when she was young that she thought she would like to be a hairstylist or maybe a psychologist when she grew up, because she liked talking to people.

She also sang and put on little shows for the women in the salon. She was interested in all kinds of music, including rock, reggae, R&B (rhythm and blues), and African rhythms. She also loved and admired British-Nigerian singer Sade, who was one of her favorite artists. Beyoncé was drawn to any activity that allowed her to be creative, including dancing, singing, writing songs and poems, drawing, and painting.

Little Sister

Solange Piaget Knowles was born on June 24, 1986, in Houston, Texas. Like her older sister, she is a recording artist, actress, model, and fashion designer. In her teens, Solange occasionally worked with Destiny's Child, including a stint as a replacement backup dancer during a tour. She also filled in for Kelly Rowland in 2000 after Rowland broke two toes.

At age 16, she was chosen to sing the theme song to the Disney Channel TV show *The Proud Family* and was backed by Destiny's Child. In addition, she often appeared as a backup performer with other acts, including Kelly Rowland and Lil' Romeo.

In 2003, Solange released her first album, *Solo Star*. She released her second album, *Sol-Angel and the Hadley St. Dreams* in 2008, which received a better response than her first, debuting at number nine on the U.S. Billboard 200 chart. In 2012, she released her *True* EP. She topped the Billboard 200 chart in 2016 with her third studio album, *A Seat at the Table*, which features the songs "Cranes in the Sky" and "Don't Touch My Hair."

In February 2004, a 17-year-old Solange married her childhood sweetheart, football player Daniel Smith. The couple had a son, Daniel Julez Smith Jr. In October 2007, Solange revealed in an interview with *Essence* magazine that the couple had divorced.

Quality Family Time

The Knowles family spent a lot of family time together, especially Sundays, which were family days for them. A regular family event was the rodeo. Every year, Tina and Mathew would take Beyoncé and Solange to the Houston Livestock Show and

for her family and at her mother's hair salon, she was extremely shy, and this affected her at school. Although she was a good student, she rarely raised her hand in class. She would shrink down in her seat whenever her teachers called on her. She kept to herself and tried hard to avoid attention.

There was another reason aside from shyness that Beyoncé wished to escape notice. Her classmates teased her about a number of things, including her name. Although she has since grown to love her first name, when she was a child, she hated it because it gave the other kids a reason to tease her.

The teasing eventually began to interfere with her self-confidence. For example, she had always loved math, recalling, "It was fun for me, sort of like figuring out riddles … I was always fascinated by how complicated it looked and how simple it really was."[7] By seventh grade, however, the higher-level math became more challenging for her, and she struggled to understand it. A boy who sat next to her in math class called her dumb and ugly, and she began to believe him.

The teasing she endured at school led her to feel insecure about her body and intelligence, and it eroded her self-esteem. It also made her feel like she did not fit in with the other kids at school. "I've always been the type of person who cares so much about what everybody thinks, to the point where it was kind of sick," Beyoncé has said. "Like it messed with my head, my self-esteem."[8] She became even more introverted, and her quietness made some of her classmates think she was a snob.

At age nine, she switched to Parker Elementary School, a music magnet school in Houston, and joined the school's choir. She also sang in the choir at her family's church, St. John's United Methodist Church. In the eighth grade, she attended a public school for one year, Welch Middle School. She had heard frightening stories from a cousin about how tough the other girls were and that they would be jealous of her pretty, long hair and cut it off, so she wore her hair in a bun for a year. Beyoncé went on to attend the High School for the Performing and Visual Arts in Houston, where she no longer felt threatened by school bullies, but she left school in ninth grade to be homeschooled.

Gaining Confidence

Beyoncé's parents worried about her low self-esteem and her shyness in public. One way they tried to help her improve her self-image was by enrolling her in dance lessons to study ballet and jazz dancing. Her parents knew she enjoyed dancing. In fact, she began dancing as a youngster even before she began walking. They thought that dancing would help her gain more confidence in her body and become less self-conscious.

Beyoncé's dance teacher, a woman named Darlette Johnson, played a large role in shaping her life. One day when Beyoncé was the last child to be picked up from dance lessons, Johnson started singing. When Beyoncé joined in with her, Johnson was amazed by her ability to hit the high notes. She urged Beyoncé to enter the St. Mary's talent show, even though Beyoncé was always terrified before school performances. Johnson recalled, "She would literally have tears in her eyes. I would have to hold on to her and tell her, it's okay, take deep breaths."[9] When Beyoncé took the stage at the talent show, however, the seven-year-old came alive. As soon as the music started and she began to sing, she was instantly more confident, poised, and in command of herself. Beyoncé said, "I'm not sure where I found the courage. All I know is that I felt at home on that stage, more so than anywhere else."[10] As she sang the John Lennon classic "Imagine," her parents were astounded. Although they knew she liked to sing, they had not heard her rehearse the song before the show. They both realized that their daughter was musically gifted, and they could not believe the girl onstage was the same shy child they knew.

Beyoncé was nominated for a local talent award for her performance in the show. After receiving such high recognition for her talent, she began entering singing and dancing competitions on a regular basis. She loved performing but did not enjoy dressing up for the beauty portion of the competitions. Beyoncé was always a bit of a tomboy and preferred wearing pants and loose-fitting shirts as a child, but for the competitions, she had to put on frilly dresses and makeup. She also had to model on a runway for the judges and the audience. Once again, her shyness dissolved when she was onstage, and she would strut around the runway like a professional model and even blow a kiss to the audience. Beyoncé won first place in so many of the competitions that her tiny bedroom was stuffed full of awards and trophies.

Then one day in 1990, when Beyoncé was nine, she went to a talent show that would change her life. This annual contest was sponsored by the People's Workshop for the Visual and Performing Arts, a nonprofit group that showcased talented children in the Houston area. After Beyoncé's performance, two women from the audience approached her and asked whether she would like to join an all-girl group that they were putting together. Beyoncé attended auditions, along with about 60 other girls in Houston. When Beyoncé was chosen for the group, it marked the beginning of her professional career.

First Girl Group

The name of the group was Girl's Tyme. Beyoncé became the lead singer in this pop and R&B group. Girl's Tyme had an ever-changing lineup of 5 to 7 members, with nearly 100 second- and third-grade girls rotating through it over the years. They performed at places and events in Houston, including the Miss Black Houston Pageant, Six Flags AstroWorld, banquets, rodeos, festivals, and high school concerts. Soon, they had a manager, a woman named Andretta Tillman. She would have the girls watch videos of other famous girl groups performing, including two very successful ones, the Supremes and En Vogue. The girls studied these performers so they could imitate their singing style and the way they moved on stage.

Beyoncé became good friends with two of the other members of Girl's Tyme, LaTavia Roberson and Kelly Rowland. Beyoncé and Kelly were especially close. Kelly's mother worked as a live-in nanny and traveled frequently, so Kelly, who was nearly always at Beyoncé's house rehearsing anyway, soon moved in with the Knowles family. Kelly became like a second sister to Beyoncé. They shared a bedroom, a bathroom, the telephone, and even clothes. The two of them rehearsed with each other and with the other girls constantly, practicing their singing and dancing moves in Beyoncé's bedroom and backyard and at Tina's hair salon. Kelly

A Father's Influence

Mathew Knowles is widely recognized as the driving force behind Destiny's Child. Although today he is a multimillionaire, he grew up poor. His father was a truck driver, and his mother worked as a maid. Their home in Alabama did not have indoor plumbing, and the family used an outhouse. In addition to struggling with poverty, they faced racism. Knowles grew up in the 1950s and early 1960s, when the South was still segregated, meaning that blacks and whites used separate facilities. Thanks to his mother's activism, Knowles became the first black student to attend his junior high school and one of the first to attend his high school.

Taking his cue from his mother, Knowles became involved in the civil rights movement in his teens. During the 1960s, he marched in demonstrations and participated in sit-ins, in which black customers sat in whites-only establishments and refused to leave until they were served. Knowles was one of the first black students at the University of Tennessee at Chattanooga and later

and the other members of the group spent so much time at the Knowles house that Beyoncé has described this period as being "like eternal summer camp."[11]

In 1991, Beyoncé suggested that the group include her friend LeToya Luckett, with whom Beyoncé had appeared in the school play *Pinocchio*. Now a six-person group, Girl's Tyme continued to perform at local events. The girls were hoping to get a record deal some day. Then, in 1993, they got a big break. They sent a videotape of themselves performing to the TV show *Star Search*, which was a popular talent competition. Over the years, many *Star Search* contestants went on to become big stars, including Britney Spears, Christina Aguilera, and Justin Timberlake. The

switched to Fisk University, a historically black college in Nashville, Tennessee. He graduated in 1974 with degrees in economics and management. His experiences confronting injustice, as well as his strong work ethic and business acumen, have deeply influenced his daughters.

Mathew Knowles has taught seminars on the entertainment industry.

girls were elated when they were invited to appear on the show. Beyoncé's mother helped out by creating satin jackets for the girls to pair with colorful shorts.

The group members decided on a rap song for their appearance. Although they were well prepared and performed smoothly, the rap song did not show off their strongest talent, which was their vocal harmonizing. Unfortunately for Girl's Tyme, the judges chose a rock band as the winner that night. After their loss, Beyoncé and the other girls ran from the stage with tears in their eyes. This early experience shaped Beyoncé and taught her to show resilience in the face of defeat and turn her disappointment into determination to achieve success. She would recognize these early moments later as learning opportunities and building blocks that helped her reach the next level of her career. Little did she know, she would have more ahead of her than she could ever imagine.

Beyoncé's early experiences struggling to gain exposure as an artist allowed her to develop a thick skin and prepared her for a career in the entertainment industry.

Chapter Two

Finding Success with Destiny's Child

Moving forward with her role in Girl's Tyme, Beyoncé was determined to succeed. Luckily for the group, the other members shared her mentality, and their top priority became acquiring a recording contract. While they knew it would require a lot of hard work to achieve, they were up to the task. Beyoncé's father, Mathew Knowles, played a crucial role in managing, shaping, and promoting the girls' act. He was one of the main reasons Girl's Tyme gained recognition and eventually evolved into Destiny's Child. The latter became one of the most successful music groups ever, with multiple Grammy Awards and a star on the Hollywood Walk of Fame. However, this success didn't come without the occasional downfall.

Performance Boot Camp

Mathew Knowles believed Girl's Tyme had enough talent to become successful, and he vowed to help them secure a recording contract. After their loss on *Star Search* in 1993, he made an important decision: He quit his job as a salesman to devote himself full-time to the girls. He served as co-manager along with Andretta Tillman until her death in 1997, when he took over as sole manager of the group.

Mathew initiated a number of changes in the group, including their lineup and name. He changed the group's focus from dancing to singing and reduced the number of members from the six who had appeared on *Star Search* to four. The group now consisted of Beyoncé, Kelly Rowland, LaTavia Roberson, and LeToya Luckett. The group tried out several different names over the next few years, including Something Fresh, Borderline, Cliché, Self Expression, and the Dolls. Then one day, Tina came across the word "destiny" while reading a passage from the Bible and thought that it was an appropriate name, so they went by that for several years. In addition to the name and lineup changes, the girls experimented with different musical styles, including hip-hop, gospel, and R&B.

One of the most valuable contributions that Mathew made to the group was instituting a performance "boot camp" to train the girls in dancing and singing. Every summer for three years, from the time they were preteens until they were in their early teens, the girls attended Mathew's boot camp. He set a strict schedule for them. They started their day with a 3-mile (4.8 km) run through Memorial Park in Houston to get them in shape. In addition, he had them sing while they jogged in order to build up their endurance and develop the stamina required to sing and dance at the same time. After

The original lineup of Destiny's Child (shown here) did not include Michelle Williams, who was added later.

their run, the girls would practice singing and dancing for hours. They practiced all day long in the summers, and during the school year, they would rehearse on Saturdays from around 2:00 p.m. until midnight. They also continued to watch videos of successful singing groups such as the Supremes and the Jackson 5. The boot camp also focused on a healthy diet.

As part of his boot camp, Mathew built a wooden stage in the backyard. He hired a professional model to teach the girls how to walk in high heels and become more poised. Mathew gave them tips on what to say on stage between songs, as well as on how to answer questions from reporters. They would practice this bantering and interviewing by role-playing with Mathew and each other.

First Record Deal

Mathew wanted the girls to become more comfortable on stage performing in front of an audience. So he set a goal for the group to perform at one event per week during the school year and two per week during the summer. Beyoncé spent a great deal of time in her preteen and early teen years either practicing or performing in her backyard and at her mother's hair salon. Like her father and the other girls in the group, she was determined to get a recording contract and create a hit album.

Soon, the group began appearing as the opening act for established performers and groups, including Christina Aguilera, SWV, Dru Hill, and Immature. They also continued to compete in talent shows and competitions throughout Texas. In between these appearances, they created and mailed out demo tapes and photographs of themselves to record companies. While Mathew looked for performance venues for the girls, Tina served as the group's hairstylist and costume designer. Tina's one-of-a-kind creations included coordinated outfits made of colorful satin and lace embellished with sequins and beads.

In 1995, all their hard work finally began to pay off. Daryl Simmons, a representative from Silent Partner Productions, heard the group perform and was impressed. He contacted Mathew and offered the group a recording contract. The group, which was

Tina Knowles Lawson

Tina Knowles Lawson's background had a huge impact on Beyoncé's destiny as a performer. Born Célestine Ann Beyincé, Tina grew up in Galveston, Texas, where she attended a Catholic elementary school. Tina's mother was an accomplished seamstress who sewed for her family and for others. In fact, her mother paid for part of Tina's tuition by making vestments for the altar boys and priests at their church. "My mother was so talented and so resourceful. People would come to her to make their prom dresses and beautiful formal gowns," Tina said. "Her creations were often embellished with hand-smocking, beading, lace, embroidery and jeweled buttons."[1]

In junior high, Tina joined an all-girl singing group named the Veltones, which was modeled after 1960s girl groups such as the Supremes. Tina used what she had learned from her mother about sewing to design costumes for the group, which sang at local events in Galveston. These experiences came in handy years later when her own daughter, Beyoncé, joined an all-girl

then called the Dolls, had finally reached their goal of securing a record deal. With LaTavia's mother as a chaperone, the four girls moved to Atlanta, Georgia, where Silent Partner was located, to begin recording.

It was the first time Beyoncé had been away from her family, and although she missed them, she and the other girls had a great time in Atlanta. They were paid $150 a week, most of which they spent at department stores on clothing. They slept on cots and a couch in the basement of Simmons's assistant and were tutored in regular schoolwork in the mornings. In the afternoons, they recorded their songs.

singing group. Tina not only gave her daughter advice on how to perform on stage, she also designed and created unique costumes for Beyoncé and the other members of Destiny's Child.

1. Quoted in Warner Roberts, "Tina Knowles: Pop Star's Mom Sews Some Diva-licious Threads," H-Texas, September 1, 2007. htexas.com/edit/tina-knowles.

Tina Knowles Lawson is known for starting her House of Deréon and Miss Tina by Tina Knowles fashion brands.

Only eight months after signing them, however, the label dropped the girls. Silent Partner had decided not to put any more money into the group. Being let go after thinking they had finally made it was a shock to the girls and another huge disappointment. "It was like *Star Search* all over again,"[12] Beyoncé recalled.

Becoming Destiny's Child

After their record deal with Silent Partner Productions fell through, the girls did not give up. They returned to Houston, where they continued to practice and make public appearances. Then in 1996, the girls got another chance at a deal when Columbia Records invited them to fly to New York for an audition. Even though the roomful of music executives were welcoming, the girls were nervous when they sang their two audition songs, "Are You Ready?" and "Ain't No Sunshine," a cappella (without musical accompaniment). After they finished singing, Beyoncé and the others could not tell from the executives' facial expressions what they thought of the girls' performance. The girls returned to Houston, where they waited for weeks to hear back about their audition.

Then one day, the girls were in Tina's hair salon when Beyoncé's parents handed them an envelope. Inside was a recording contract from Columbia Records—and the realization of a lifelong dream for the girls. When the four of them saw the contract, they started crying and screaming. Beyoncé recalled, "The ladies with their heads under the dryers looked at us like we were crazy …

LaTavia, Beyoncé, and Kelly (from left to right) are shown here performing on stage at one of their early shows.

We ran all around the shop, jumping up and down, holding our contract in the air for all the customers to see."[13]

When the girls signed with Columbia, they were known as Destiny. One final name change was in order, however. When they were asked to contribute a song to the soundtrack of the 1997 movie *Men in Black*, Mathew discovered that there were literally dozens of groups named Destiny, so he added "Child" to distinguish them from the other groups, and they became Destiny's Child.

First Hit Singles and Album

When Destiny's Child contributed the song "Killing Time" to the *Men in Black* soundtrack, they were still unknown to the public. That changed with the release of their debut album, *Destiny's Child*, in 1998. Beyoncé and the other girls cowrote two of the songs for this self-titled album, which the legendary musician Wyclef Jean helped produce. The album contained the single "No, No, No Part 1." However, it was the remix of the song, "No, No, No Part 2," which featured Jean on vocals, that became a hit single. The song went straight to the top of the Billboard Hot R&B/Hip-Hop Songs chart and sold more than 1 million copies worldwide.

"No, No, No Part 2" helped the group earn its first awards. The song won two Soul Train Lady of Soul Awards and helped propel sales of the album. *Destiny's Child* peaked at number 6 on the UK R&B Albums chart and was certified platinum by the Recording Industry Association of America (RIAA), having sold more than 1 million copies in the United States. The album also garnered the group a third Soul Train Lady of Soul Award, this one for Best R&B/Soul Album of the Year.

On the heels of the success of their debut album, the group wasted no time getting back into the studio to record their second album. Beyoncé, Kelly, LaTavia, and LeToya took more control of this album, cowriting 11 of the album's 14 songs and serving as coproducers. Released in 1999, *The Writing's on the Wall* performed even better than their first album. It produced 4 number 1 hit singles: "Bills, Bills, Bills," "Bug a Boo," "Jumpin', Jumpin'," and "Say My Name." *The Writing's on the Wall* went

8 times platinum after selling more than 8 million copies. In 2001, the group was nominated for multiple Grammy Awards, including Record of the Year, and won two of the coveted awards for the song "Say My Name."

In addition to the awards she won with Destiny's Child, Beyoncé was deeply honored to win the 2001 Songwriter of the Year award from the American Society of Composers, Authors, and Publishers. She was the second woman and the first black woman ever to win the award. This accomplishment is all the more notable because she was not yet 20 years old when she won the award. "I love writing songs because it's like therapy," Beyoncé said, "but sometimes when you're trying to write a hit song, it's not fun at all. When you write because you have something to say, that's when great things come out."[14]

Losing Original Members

Despite the phenomenal success of the group's second album, *The Writing's on the Wall* would be the last by Destiny's Child to feature all four of the original members. Tension had been building for some time because LaTavia and LeToya felt like outsiders in the group. Beyoncé's father managed the group, and Beyoncé and Kelly were close friends. LaTavia and LeToya also thought Beyoncé was getting more attention from the media than the others in the group were and that Mathew Knowles was unfairly promoting his daughter over them.

Soon after *The Writing's on the Wall* was released, LaTavia and LeToya sent identical letters to Mathew, Beyoncé, and Kelly, saying that they no longer wanted Mathew to manage their careers. Beyoncé, who had always seen herself as a peacemaker, felt caught in the middle between her two good friends and her father, and she tried desperately to make things work out for everyone. The four young women even sought counseling with their youth minister at church. However, the problems within the group ran deep, and nothing they tried helped. Mathew Knowles wound up firing LaTavia and LeToya in December 1999. The two women then filed a lawsuit against him, accusing him of breach of contract, keeping more than his share of the profits, and unfairly favoring Beyoncé and Kelly over them.

In addition to their lawsuit against Knowles, LaTavia and LeToya also filed suit against Beyoncé for defamation of character after she commented to the media on the situation. This lawsuit was eventually dropped, with Beyoncé agreeing not to speak publicly about the group's problems. It was a very difficult time for her. Some Destiny's Child fans blamed her for the problems in the group, and she had to endure hate mail as well as accusations and gossip in the tabloids and on the internet.

Heartbreak and Depression

The lawsuit against Mathew Knowles was eventually settled out of court, but the stress of this time took a huge toll on Beyoncé. In addition to the group's problems, she was going through her first breakup with a boyfriend. She had dated a boy named Lindell for six years and had attended his high school prom with him. Things began to change between them once Destiny's Child became successful and Beyoncé had more demands on her time—and less time to spend with Lindell. "After I left school to start recording, dating got kind of hard," she explained. "We didn't see each other all that much."[15] By the time she was 18, their long romance had come to an end, although they remained on friendly terms.

In the midst of all this stress, 18-year-old Beyoncé became very depressed and developed acne for the first time in her life. Without the emotional support of her longtime boyfriend to help her cope with everything, she stayed in her bedroom for days, not talking to anyone. "I was unhappy," she says. "I hated the way I looked. I hated everything that was going on. There was so much tension in my house, because my whole house was Destiny's Child."[16]

Beyoncé turned to her deep faith in God and managed to recover from her period of depression. She even found some closure with LaTavia and LeToya, telling them she was sorry for all their problems and that she forgave them. The experience helped her gain a more mature perspective on life and become a stronger woman. "I became an entirely different person after that," she said. "My whole way of thinking and dealing with things changed."[17]

Final Lineup

Although Destiny's Child had lost two members, the group still had concerts and public appearances to honor. In addition, they still had to make the video for the song "Say My Name," which had already been choreographed and arranged for four performers. With all this in mind, Mathew hired two performers to replace LaTavia and LeToya: Michelle Williams and Farrah Franklin. Both had some professional experience: Michelle had sung backup for the singer Monica, and Farrah had been in a singing group and had performed as a backup dancer in the Destiny's Child music video for the song "Bills, Bills, Bills."

Since the vocals had already been laid down for "Say My Name," Michelle and Farrah lip-synched to LaTavia's and LeToya's voices for the video. The two new members then embarked with Beyoncé and Kelly on a whirlwind of promotional activities that included an Australian tour. It was all a bit overwhelming for Farrah Franklin, who began to miss practices. On the day of the group's flight to Australia, Farrah did not show up at the airport. Beyoncé called her and tried to coax her into coming, telling her it was unprofessional of her not to fulfill her obligations. The result of the phone call was that after only five months, Franklin was out of the group, and Destiny's Child was now a trio.

The group had been through some tough times, and now Beyoncé and Kelly were all that remained of the original Destiny's Child lineup. However, once again, Beyoncé acknowledged that the difficulties helped her grow and mature as a person. She, Kelly, and Michelle learned a lot about themselves and each other in the midst of all this turmoil. "We've learned about loyalty," Beyoncé noted, "about the importance of loving and caring about the people in the group, sticking together, how to be a friend, how to apologize when you're wrong, and how to compromise."[18]

The final lineup of Destiny's Child was (from left to right) Kelly Rowland, Beyoncé Knowles, and Michelle Williams.

Survivor *and Hiatus*

In 2001, Destiny's Child produced its third album, *Survivor*. Beyoncé got the name for the album when she heard a disc jockey (DJ) joking on the air about the members of Destiny's Child voting each other off, as contestants do on the TV reality show *Survivor*. The album featured all three women singing lead, and it debuted in the number 1 spot on the Billboard 200 chart. It was one of the best-selling albums in the history of Columbia Records and went on to be certified quadruple platinum by the RIAA. The album earned Destiny's Child more Grammy nominations, and the group won for Best R&B Performance by a Duo or Group with Vocals for the song "Survivor."

Billboard magazine eventually ranked the *Survivor* album at number 70 on its Top 200 Albums of the Decade list. After all the lineup changes and drama-filled altercations between the members of Destiny's Child, the group was ready for a break. Beyoncé,

Destiny's Child is shown here performing in 2001.

Kelly, and Michelle were all in agreement and announced the group was going on hiatus (a break from recording and touring) and each member was going to be free to pursue solo projects. These were the first steps Beyoncé took to beginning her solo career, which would later prove to bring her an even higher level of success and millions more devoted fans.

Chapter Three

Becoming a Solo Artist

Beyoncé made the decision to pursue a solo career while also exploring other avenues of her creativity in the three years that Destiny's Child was on hiatus. In this time, she grew as an independent performer, starred in three movies, and released her debut solo album, which was well received by the public. When Destiny's Child came back together to record their fourth and final album, Beyoncé was already a sensation all on her own.

Carmen: A Hip Hopera

The MTV cable network asked Beyoncé to star in the movie *Carmen: A Hip Hopera*. This 2001 musical was based on the 1875 opera *Carmen* by French composer Georges Bizet and updated to take place in modern times in Philadelphia, Pennsylvania, and Los Angeles, California. The movie features an all-black cast and hip-hop/R&B music instead of Bizet's original musical score.

Beyoncé played Carmen Brown, the title character, who is an aspiring actress—much like Beyoncé herself. However, their personalities are nothing alike. Carmen is a devious and manipulative femme fatale, whereas Beyoncé is polite and often

Kelly Rowland's Life and Career

Kelly Rowland has had two Grammy Award–winning hits since the disbanding of Destiny's Child. The first was in 2002, when she won a Grammy for "Dilemma," a collaboration with rapper Nelly. She won again in 2009 for collaborating with French DJ and music producer David Guetta on the single "When Love Takes Over." In 2010, she and Guetta collaborated again on "Commander," which also became a hit song. She also received a Grammy nomination for her 2011 song "Motivation," which features rapper Lil Wayne. She has released four solo albums as of late 2018: 2002's *Simply Deep*, 2007's *Ms. Kelly*, 2011's *Here I Am*, and 2013's *Talk a Good Game*.

Rowland has done some acting as well. She had a supporting role in the 2003 horror film *Freddy vs. Jason* and starred in the 2004 romantic comedy *The Seat Filler*. In 2012, she played a role in the romantic comedy *Think Like a Man,* and in 2017, she was featured in the made-for-TV movie *Love by the 10th Date*. She has also made guest appearances on TV sitcoms. In 2011, she became a judge on the British reality TV music competition show *The X Factor*, and in 2013, she became a judge on the final season of *The X Factor USA*.

In May 2014, Rowland married her manager Tim Witherspoon in Costa Rica. The couple welcomed

considered a role model. Playing a part that was so different from her own personality was a real challenge for Beyoncé, especially considering she was only 19 years old and this was her first acting role.

Neither of her parents came to Los Angeles for the filming.

their first child, Titan Jewell Witherspoon, that same year on November 4. Beyoncé and Kelly, who have been close since childhood, now both have children of their own and connect on an even deeper level: "They are extremely close," Rowland said referring to Beyoncé's daughter Blue Ivy and her son Titan. "It's the sweetest thing. It's the greatest thing about friendship when you're able to grow up together and your children are able to grow up together and it's just years upon years of beautiful friendship and sisterhood."[1]

Kelly Rowland's 2013 album, *Talk a Good Game*, landed at number 4 on the Billboard 200 chart.

1. Quoted in Natalie Finn, "Inside Beyoncé's Inner Circle: A Look at the Most Important Relationships in Her Life," Eonline .com, February 8, 2017. www.eonline.com/ news/827091/ inside-beyonce-s- inner-circle-a-look-at- the-most-important- relationships-in-her-life.

She didn't have her mother there to get her up in the morning and make her breakfast or her father to give her advice or help make decisions. This was one of the first times Beyoncé was responsible for herself in an adult way. "I appreciated the chance it gave me to learn more about myself," she said.

"Suddenly I was making up my own mind and learning to trust my judgment."[19]

Beyoncé grew up a lot while making the movie and learned to be more self-sufficient. Since the beginning of her singing career, she had been part of girl groups where she had become used to functioning as part of a unit. Now, on the set of *Carmen*, she had to learn to function as an individual. This meant speaking up for her needs rather than compromising with others in order to keep the peace. "I've learned something about myself outside of Destiny's Child," Beyoncé said at the time. "Movies are my college, my time to go and discover."[20]

When the movie aired on MTV in May 2001, film critics were impressed by Beyoncé's performance. A movie reviewer for *Variety* said she turned out "a fine acting debut" and added that Beyoncé "makes it clear that she's got a surplus of star power."[21]

Goldmember

Soon after making her acting debut in *Carmen*, Beyoncé was surprised by an offer of another script. This time, the script was for the 2002 feature film *Austin Powers in Goldmember*, the third installment in the *Austin Powers* series, starring actor and comedian Mike Myers. Whereas her role in *Carmen* involved a lot of singing, the role she would play in *Goldmember*—that of Foxxy Cleopatra—required more acting than singing. This made Beyoncé feel nervous and intimidated during the audition process. She was so afraid she would say the wrong thing, in fact, that she did not speak much outside of reading her lines. When one of the movie's producers asked her how she felt about appearing in a comedy, the ever-honest and straightforward Beyoncé told him that she was not sure whether she could be funny—and then worried that the comment had blown her chances of getting the role. "That's probably not what you should tell a Hollywood producer who is thinking about casting you in their multimillion-dollar comedy,"[22] she confessed later.

Despite her candor, Beyoncé was offered the role of Foxxy

Beyoncé is shown here at the *Goldmember* premiere in 2002.

Cleopatra the next day. She earned $3 million for her portrayal of the tough-talking, 1970s-era secret agent Foxxy. She found the character she played in *Goldmember* to be sweeter and easier to portray than that of Carmen. Whereas Carmen was very different from her, Foxxy Cleopatra had a side that Beyoncé felt very comfortable with. As she noted, "I can relate a lot to her, because she's really strong and sassy and she has got a lot of soul."[23]

While she felt mostly comfortable with the role, some aspects of acting still made her uneasy. Although this was her second movie, she was still very inexperienced, and this made her feel insecure about her work during the filming. She found that remembering her lines and performing her character's movements in the right place—called hitting your mark—to be a challenge:

I have a tough time recalling the lyrics to songs that I've written

*myself, even after singing them hundreds of times! Now I have to
remember the exact words from a script I only got a few weeks
ago, while also kicking down a door and pulling out a gun on the
bad guy. I also have to make sure that I'm standing in the correct
spot, and then I need to count how many steps I'm supposed to
take to hit my next mark.*[24]

Fortunately for her, director Jay Roach and the rest of the
cast were very supportive and helped her feel more comfortable on the set. She and Myers got along well on the set, and
she was grateful for the opportunity to learn from him.

Beyoncé recorded several songs for the movie's soundtrack,
including the 1970s-disco-inspired title track for the movie,
"Hey Goldmember," and her debut solo single, "Work It Out."
The movie opened at number 1 at the box office and grossed
more than $296 million worldwide. Despite its good showing
at the box office, it received mixed reviews from film critics,
as did Beyoncé's performance. Roger Ebert was one reviewer
who liked the character of Foxxy Cleopatra and her "Afro out
to there" but was disappointed that "the movie doesn't do
much with her except assign her to look extremely good while
standing next to Austin."[25]

Playing Lilly

The following year, Beyoncé got a chance to try something
different when she starred in the musical dramedy *The Fighting
Temptations*. She appeared opposite Cuba Gooding Jr., whose
character must revive a gospel choir in order to collect an
inheritance. Beyoncé played the role of Lilly, a single mother
and lounge singer who joins the choir. The role gave Beyoncé
a chance to play a character whose life was different from her
own, because Lilly is an unwed mother who is looked upon
unfavorably by others in her small town.

The movie gave her a chance to go in a different direction
musically as well: She performed songs in the movie that were
different from the type she sang with Destiny's Child. "I'm

doing serious old-school hymns, and I get to do some really soulful, funky stuff,"[26] she commented. She recorded several songs that received positive acclaim, including the gospel hymn "Swing Low, Sweet Chariot" and a version of the classic tune "Fever."

The movie received lackluster reviews, as most reviewers found the plot weak and predictable. *The Fighting Temptations* was also not as financially successful as Beyoncé's first two movies.

Debut Album

Even though her films were not all box office hits, Beyoncé felt she had gained valuable acting experience from working on them. With three movies to her credit, she decided it was time to return to the recording studio. In 2002 and 2003, she recorded her debut solo album *Dangerously in Love*. The album, which was released in June 2003, contained 15 songs cowritten and coproduced by Beyoncé. It sold more than 317,000 copies in its first week and debuted at number 1 on the Billboard 200 chart. Within a month, it had sold more than 1 million copies and was certified platinum by the RIAA. It went on to be certified quadruple platinum after selling more than 4 million copies.

The album's songs were a mix of hip-hop, soul, and R&B. Several musicians lent their star power to the album by collaborating on lyrics, music, and vocals, including rapper JAY-Z (whose real name is Shawn Carter). Beyoncé had met the rapper and hip-hop mogul in 2002 when she recorded the duet "'03 Bonnie & Clyde" with him for his album *The Blueprint*[2]. Now, JAY-Z returned the favor by contributing to the songs "That's How You Like It" and "Crazy in Love" on Beyoncé's debut album. Beyoncé was working on the lyrics and music for "Crazy in Love" and got stuck, thinking it needed something more to spice it up. She asked JAY-Z for advice, and he added some rap lyrics, which he performed during the recording session. The duet was the lead single from the album and became Beyoncé's first number 1 single as a solo artist.

Dangerously in Love was nominated for five Grammy Awards.

It was a huge honor to be nominated for so many Grammys for her first solo album, but on the night of the 2004 Grammy Awards show, Beyoncé joined the ranks of an elite few when she tied a record by winning all five Grammys for which she had been nominated. She tied Alicia Keys, Norah Jones, and Lauryn Hill for the most Grammys won by a female artist in a single night. During her acceptance speech for the Best Contemporary R&B Album award, Beyoncé said, "This is unbelievable ... I'm just so honored. I want to thank the Grammys for giving me this wonderful opportunity." She added breathlessly, "This was my first record as a solo artist!"[27]

Beyoncé and JAY-Z performed together on MTV's TRL in 2002.

Dating Rumors

"Crazy in Love" stayed at number 1 on the Billboard chart for eight weeks, and the video received a lot of airplay. JAY-Z's contribution to the lyrics for this hit song, as well as his appearance in the song's video, helped to fuel rumors of a romantic relationship between him and Beyoncé. The rumors had been swirling ever since their first collaboration.

In fact, Beyoncé and JAY-Z did begin dating after their first collaboration. The two got along well and had a lot in common, even though he is 12 years older than she is. They were frequently photographed together at basketball games, parties, fashion shows, concerts, and restaurants. The media reported numerous rumors about them, including that they were engaged, that she was pregnant, and that they had secretly married. There were even rumors that JAY-Z had taken over as her manager. Through it all, however, both Beyoncé and JAY-Z did not talk about their relationship in interviews. During one interview, Beyoncé responded to the suggestion that it might put a stop to some of the persistent rumors if she would just talk about her romantic life: "I just like to feel that I have something to myself," she explained. "I'm a singer, I'll talk about writing songs all you want. But when it comes to certain personal things any normal person wouldn't tell people they don't know, I just feel like I don't have to [talk about it]."[28]

Destiny's Final Album

To promote *Dangerously in Love*, in 2003, Beyoncé embarked on her first solo tour, appearing throughout Europe. The tour was notable for the way she entered the stage at the beginning of each concert: She was lowered onto the stage upside down while singing "Baby Boy." This unusual entrance was her idea, as she explained in an interview with a British newspaper: "I saw it in a Broadway show and it looked really cool. I do it every night, and now I'm upset because it's not fun [anymore]. I'm scared to eat too close to the time. It was OK the first time, but when you have to do it 30 times …"[29] She trailed off to make the point that hanging upside down in a harness from the ceiling of a theater night after night gets old fast.

Beyoncé's experiences touring solo, as well as her phenomenal success as a solo artist, led her to realize she could not go back to being part of a group. She, Kelly, and Michelle had

Michelle Williams's Life and Career

Michelle Williams released her first solo album, *Heart to Yours*, in 2002. This gospel and R&B album was the best-selling gospel album of that year and earned Williams a Music of Black Origin (MOBO) Award. Her second album, *Do You Know*, was released in 2004 and is similar in musical styles to her first. While it did not sell very well, it did earn her a nomination for another MOBO Award. In 2008, Williams released her first solo pop album, *Unexpected*. The album's lead single, "We Break the Dawn," reached number 1 on Billboard's Hot Dance Airplay chart. Another single, "The Greatest," reached number one on Billboard's Dance Club Songs chart. In 2014, Williams returned to her gospel and R&B roots and released her fourth solo album, *Journey to Freedom*. The album peaked at number 2 on Billboard's Top Gospel Albums chart. Beyoncé and Kelly featured on the album's song "Say Yes," which reached number 1 on Billboard's Hot Gospel Songs chart.

Williams also tried her hand at acting. In 2003, she made her stage debut in the lead role in the musical *Aida*, becoming the only former Destiny's Child member to appear on Broadway as of 2019. Next, in 2007, she

each embarked on solo projects, and now they all agreed it was time to bring Destiny's Child to an end. They reconnected to release one last album and say goodbye to all their fans. After three years apart, the members of Destiny's Child recorded and released their fourth and final album, *Destiny Fulfilled*, in 2004. One clear indication of the impact of their individual played the role of Shug Avery in *The Color Purple*. From 2009 to 2010, she played Roxie Hart in the London and Broadway productions of the musical *Chicago*. She also starred in David E. Talbert's stage play *What My Husband Doesn't Know* in 2012. In 2013, she played the role of Sandra Isadore in *Fela!* Williams has also made guest appearances on television, including as a featured judge on *MTV's Top Pop Group* in 2008, as a contestant on the British dance competition *Strictly Come Dancing* in 2010, and with Deitrick Haddon on the Oxygen reality television series *Fix My Choir*.

Williams has been open about her struggles with depression throughout her life, including during her time in Destiny's Child.

careers is the fact that each member contributed equally to the writing and production of the album, and the three women all served as executive producers along with Mathew Knowles.

The album received mixed reviews, with one reviewer complaining that it was filled with "exquisitely executed but ultimately dull ballads."[30] However, their fans disagreed with this review, and *Destiny Fulfilled* reached the number 2 spot on the U.S. Billboard 200 chart and was certified triple platinum by the RIAA.

The End of an Era

Destiny's Child's final tour appearance as a group came in September 2005 at a concert in Vancouver, British Columbia, on their Destiny Fulfilled... and Lovin' It Tour. At the end of this last show, backup dancers handed each of the three women a bouquet of flowers. Beyoncé, Kelly, and Michelle held each other in a long embrace and then turned teary-eyed to wave at the audience. "Destiny's Child started when we were nine years old," Beyoncé announced. "This isn't something somebody [just] put together. This is love."[31]

Destiny's Child became one of the best-selling female groups of all time. At the time of their breakup, they had worldwide sales of 40 million albums and singles. The group had been nominated for 14 Grammy Awards and had won three and were honored in 2006 with a star on the Hollywood Walk of

Destiny's Child's final tour came to an end in 2005.

Fame. Saying goodbye was bittersweet for each member of the group, but they all decided it was best for each of them in order to pursue their respective futures. The amount of fame and success Beyoncé achieved with Destiny's Child was impressive, yet she had no idea how many opportunities lay ahead for her as a solo artist. While she was still getting used to the idea of having a solo career, she was ready to commit to it in full force and show everyone her true star power.

Chapter Four

Owning Her Star Power

Even though Destiny's Child granted Beyoncé her first chance to shine in front of a major fan base, she knew the only way she was going to be able to achieve the level of stardom she was capable of was to split off from the group and pursue a career as a solo artist. It was not easy to stray from such a comfortable place and fellow performers that were like sisters to her, but Beyoncé knew she was meant to fulfill her own singing aspirations beyond a group dynamic.

After Destiny's Child disbanded in 2005, Beyoncé's career skyrocketed. With her next three albums, she earned multiple nominations and awards. She also continued to act, appearing in four films between 2006 and 2009: *The Pink Panther*, *Dreamgirls*, *Cadillac Records*, and *Obsessed*. She also had voice roles as Queen Tara in the 3-D computer-animated action-adventure film *Epic* in 2013 and as Nala in *The Lion King* in 2019. Beyoncé received critical acclaim for her acting, proving she was a woman of many talents who could shine in a variety of projects. Her professionalism and her achievements as a singer and an actress have earned her the right to be called a legitimately multitalented superstar.

Tying the Knot

While filming *Cadillac Records*, Beyoncé took a leap of faith and decided to marry the love of her life. After years of dodging questions in interviews about their personal relationship, Beyoncé and JAY-Z married quietly in Manhattan, New York, in April 2008. He gave her an 18-carat diamond ring valued at more than $5 million, and the ceremony took place in his penthouse. About 50 family members and close friends, including actress Gwyneth Paltrow and former bandmates Rowland and Williams, gathered for the happy occasion. The very next day, both Beyoncé and JAY-Z had to return to work—JAY-Z was touring with singer Mary J. Blige, and Beyoncé was filming *Cadillac Records*.

When Beyoncé and JAY-Z married, they each changed their last name to Knowles-Carter. This is one of the many things they had agreed upon before tying the knot. In fact, the couple put their agreements into writing in an official document known as a

Beyoncé and JAY-Z are shown here attending the 2009 Golden Globe Awards.

prenuptial agreement, or "prenup" for short. For example, in the event of their divorce, the two of them have no right to any property considered separate, such as property owned before the marriage or acquired through an inheritance. Because they both had amassed a great deal of wealth, it was important for them each to safeguard their assets in this way.

Other terms of their prenup reveal just how wealthy this power couple is. According to the agreement, Beyoncé has access to JAY-Z's $36 million private jet and his many cars, including a 1959 Rolls Royce convertible worth $1 million. If the marriage ends, JAY-Z must pay her $10 million plus another $1 million for each year they remained married for up to 15 years—meaning he could pay out as much as $25 million if they divorce. Beyoncé would also get $5 million for each pregnancy, to make up for the loss of income due to pregnancy and child rearing.

More Film Roles

Over the years, Beyoncé expanded her film roles, which helped her in gaining confidence and credibility as an actress. In 2006, she starred as Xania in *The Pink Panther*, a remake of the 1963 *Pink Panther* film. It also starred comedic actor Steve Martin as the bumbling French inspector Jacques Clouseau. *The Pink Panther* opened at number 1 at the box office and earned more than $180 million worldwide. The song "Check on It," which Beyoncé cowrote and performed for the movie, also became a number 1 hit in the United States.

Beyoncé's next movie, *Dreamgirls*, the film adaptation of the Tony Award–winning Broadway musical of the same name, tells the story of an all-girl singing group called the Dreamettes, a fictional group based on the 1960s group the Supremes. Beyoncé's character Deena Jones was based on Diana Ross, the lead singer of the Supremes. Already familiar with the performance style of the Supremes, she prepared thoroughly for her audition by spending a week watching videos of the group. She also wore a 1960s-style dress and a beehive wig to her audition, where she performed a routine. She earned the part of Deena in the cast,

Beyoncé is shown here at the Los Angeles premiere for *Dreamgirls*.

which included Jamie Foxx, Eddie Murphy, Danny Glover, Anika Noni Rose, and Jennifer Hudson. Beyoncé also cowrote one of the film's songs, "Listen." The song was nominated for several awards for best original song, including an Academy Award, and it won a Broadcast Film Critics Association Award.

In 2008, she appeared in *Cadillac Records*, the musical biopic telling the story of record company executive Leonard Chess, who sold records out of his Cadillac, and the famous artists who recorded for him. Beyoncé portrayed Etta James, the legendary blues singer who was also a heroin addict. For this role, Beyoncé gained weight and spent several weeks researching drug addiction in order to provide a more realistic portrayal of James. As part of her research, she visited the Phoenix House, a nonprofit drug and alcohol rehabilitation group in New York City where James had been treated in the 1960s. After working on the movie, Beyoncé came to idolize James: "I always loved her voice, but now knowing what she's been through, she's one of my heroes,"[32] she said. In 2010, Beyoncé won the Best Traditional R&B Vocal Performance Grammy for her version of James's "At Last" featured in the movie.

In 2009, Beyoncé portrayed a woman who was neither a singer nor a performer in the thriller *Obsessed*. Her character is a young mother whose husband is stalked by an employee at his office. The film includes a scene in which Beyoncé's character discovers that the stalker has broken into her home and a violent physical fight breaks out between the two women. The tense and extremely well-choreographed fight scene, which took more than a week to film, received high praise and won the MTV Movie Award for Best Fight.

The Brilliance of B'Day

Even though some of her films were not huge successes, Beyoncé was gaining experience and credibility on movie sets and working hard to prove herself as an actress. In the meantime, she continued writing songs for a second solo album. The album was released on September 4, 2006, Beyoncé's 25th birthday, and was titled, appropriately, *B'Day*. She cowrote every song on the album, which included funk, hip-hop, and R&B numbers. The album debuted at number 1 on the U.S.

Beyoncé traveled all over the world during her solo tour to promote *B'Day*.

Billboard 200 chart and went on to be certified triple platinum by the RIAA.

Music critics generally gave the album positive reviews. A reviewer for the *Boston Globe* praised her singing talent, saying that the album's producers helped her "focus on edgier, up-tempo tracks that take her sweet soprano to new places."[33] The album was nominated for numerous awards, including five Grammys. Like her first album, *B'Day* won the Grammy Award for Best Contemporary R&B Album.

To promote *B'Day*, Beyoncé went on a worldwide tour titled the Beyoncé Experience from April to November 2007, which received rave reviews. The tour included appearances throughout Asia, Australia, Europe, North America, and Africa. One reviewer wrote,

> [The tour] lived up to its name, with Beyonce leaving no doubt of her all-around talent. She can sing with the power of a Tina Turner, dance with the military precision of a Janet Jackson, and dress with the over-the-top flair of a Cher. More than just a concert, it's a state-of-the-art arena spectacle.[34]

Sasha Fierce Persona

Beyoncé did not waste any time in starting on her third solo album, *I Am… Sasha Fierce*, a two-disc set that she began working on in 2007. The *I Am…* side contained emotional pop ballads, such as "If I Were a Boy" and "Halo," while the *Sasha Fierce* side included more swaggering, up-tempo songs, such as "Video Phone" and "Diva." She cowrote all of the songs on the album, except "If I Were a Boy." Beyoncé created Sasha Fierce, her onstage alter ego, so she could transform herself and feel more confident while performing in front of strangers. Because she is so shy in real life, this outgoing, courageous persona helped her overcome her fears. She explained what it is like to become Sasha onstage: "I have out-of-body experiences [onstage]. If I cut my leg, if I fall, I don't even feel it. I'm so fearless, I'm not aware of my face or my body."[35] Beyoncé has insisted that for her, becoming Sasha is similar to becoming any other role she plays when acting. She has also acknowledged that Sasha is much more aggressive and overtly sexual than she is. "I'm not her in real life at all," Beyoncé said. "I'm not flirtatious and super-confident and fearless like her."[36]

The album received generally positive reviews. For example, a writer for MTV Newsroom called it "her best and boldest work yet,"[37] adding that all the tracks manage to show Beyoncé's individual twist. A reviewer for *Rolling Stone* magazine commented, "The 'Sasha' disc boasts Beyoncé's most adventurous music yet."[38] Part of the appeal of this album was the worldwide hit "Single Ladies (Put a Ring on It)," which one reviewer describes as "all bouncy hand claps and post-breakup sass."[39] The quadruple-platinum song became her biggest seller ever, and the song's video, with its unique choreography, sparked a huge dance craze and many fan tributes on YouTube. Beyoncé herself even joined in on one parody of the video on *Saturday Night Live* in November 2008, reenacting the intricate dance moves alongside Justin Timberlake, Andy Samberg, and Bobby Moynihan, all of whom wore leotards and high heels for the performance, just as Beyoncé and her dancers did in the music video.

Beyoncé performed "Single Ladies (Put a Ring on It)" at the 2008 American Music Awards in Los Angeles.

In part because of the phenomenal popularity of "Single Ladies," *I Am… Sasha Fierce* won numerous awards, including a 2009 Soul Train Music Award for Best Album of the Year. In addition, the album earned Beyoncé seven Grammy nominations. She tied her own record by winning five Grammy Awards, including Best Contemporary R&B Album. "Single Ladies" won three of these Grammys, including Song of the Year.

That same year, Beyoncé earned another special recognition for her incredible talent: *Billboard* magazine named her Woman of the Year. In making its announcement, *Billboard* said that because of her unique style, business acumen, and philanthropic efforts, Beyoncé has "not only influenced pop culture with her hit songs and signature dance moves, but has inspired women everywhere."[40] Beyoncé was thrilled by this prestigious accolade. In her acceptance speech at the ceremony, she declared, "I am the luckiest woman in the world."[41]

Taking a Year Off

After winning many awards and receiving massive amounts of recognition and praise from her fans and critics, Beyoncé made the choice to take a year off in 2010. She was constantly moving from one project to the next, and her mother stepped in and suggested she take a break from it all. "I couldn't even tell which day or which city I was at," Beyoncé said. "I would sit there at ceremonies and they would give me an award and I was just thinking about the next performance."[42] She agreed with her mom and decided this was the best choice to make to protect her mental health.

During her time off, Beyoncé visited several museums, attended ballet performances, learned how to cook, spent time with her husband, and even rode a toboggan down the Great Wall of China. She also got the chance to see JAY-Z perform from the audience's perspective, which she had never done before then. She also spent more time with her family, especially her nephew Daniel. Speaking on her break from fame, she said, "I needed some relaxation, but I wanted inspiration too, from regular everyday things. They did not have to be over-the-top productions. I was looking for tiny moments that would speak to my heart and make me smile."[43]

Old-School Charm

Beyoncé demonstrated her singing and songwriting prowess once again when she released her fourth solo album, simply titled *4*, in 2011. Like her previous albums, it debuted at number 1 on the Billboard 200 chart. The album sold 310,000 copies in its first week and was certified platinum by the RIAA in less than six weeks.

The album features R&B as well as pop music, blending 1970s R&B with 1990s rock, as well as hip-hop and soul. Beyoncé drew inspiration for the album from various artists, including Adele, the Jackson 5, and Prince. In the songs on *4*, Beyoncé's voice contains a lot of the brassiness and grittiness that appear in her live performances. The album received generally positive reviews from music critics. Reviewer Matthew Horton said that she goes "from flirty to fragile to fabulous, and is in terrific voice throughout."[44] James Reed of the *Boston Globe* agreed, writing that the album is "low-key and effortless" and that "an old-school charm breezes through several songs."[45]

This same year, she received the Billboard Millennium Award. She thanked her mother and father for teaching her about work ethic, Rowland and Williams of Destiny's Child, the original members of Destiny's Child—Luckett and Roberson—and her husband, JAY-Z.

A Multifaceted Triple Threat

The charm Beyoncé showed as a singer and songwriter on *4* is a big reason she has become a superstar. Her huge appeal as a songwriter comes from the fact that her lyrics are about things that are close to her heart—about experiences her young, mostly female fans can relate to. Beyoncé explained her goal as a songwriter: "I want people to get a better feel for who I am."[46] She writes not only about heartbreak and jealousy but also about "girl power"—women embracing themselves, taking control of their own lives, and having the strength to be independent. Jon Caramanica of the *New York Times* summed up Beyoncé's talent as a songwriter: "She has a gift for making a regular phrase indelible, as on 'Best Thing I Never Had.'"[47]

Not surprisingly, her husband, JAY-Z, also has high praise for her musical talent: "The sounds she can hear in music and memorize off of one listen are amazing. She has a wonderful ear for music—knows if people are flat, on pitch, on tone."[48] However, Beyoncé's talent and appeal extend beyond singing and songwriting. She is also a skilled dancer who studied ballet and jazz dance as a child. In addition, thanks to her father's "boot camp," she developed the ability to sing and dance at the same time while making both look effortless. A reporter for the *New York Times* said of her stage presence: "She is thunder, Beyoncé is. Fire and quake. A thing that can't quite be contained … A hard worker who makes effort look like the most glamorous thing in the world."[49]

Another thing that makes Beyoncé a true superstar is her multifaceted talent. She not only sings, writes her own songs, and dances, but she also acts, too. This versatility has ensured her place as a pop culture icon. Beyoncé demonstrates "the ability to do a movie, do a group project, then come back and do her own thing or whatever she chooses," said Erik Bradley, music director at Chicago radio station WBBM. "She is a star of stars."[50]

Woman of Style and Grace

Beyoncé's level of fame and success is due to more than just breathtaking beauty and immense talent. She is also widely admired for the graceful way she conducts herself. For example, she is known for being extremely polite. A reporter who interviewed her in 2005 for *Vanity Fair* commented, "The first thing I noticed about Beyoncé were her impeccable manners—so unusual in a big star."[51] In addition to her good manners, she has carefully cultivated her image. She has tried not to get involved in the kinds of scandals that follow many other celebrities. "It's

Taylor Swift
Acceptance Speech

One of the best known examples of Beyoncé's classiness, as well as her graciousness and generosity, occurred during an incident at the 2009 MTV Video Music Awards. That night, Beyoncé was nominated for Best Female Video for "Single Ladies," but the award went instead to Taylor Swift. When Swift took the stage to make her acceptance speech, rapper Kanye West walked onstage and took the microphone away from her and announced, "Taylor, I'm really happy for you; I'mma let you finish. But Beyoncé had one of the best videos of all time."[1] West then handed the microphone back to Swift, but the 19-year-old was too stunned to finish her speech.

Beyoncé was shocked by West's actions, but she handled the situation with grace. When she won the Best Video of the Year Award for "Single Ladies" later that evening, she walked onto the stage and announced, "I remember being seventeen years old, up for my first MTV award with Destiny's Child, and it was one of

obvious how classy she is,"[52] remarked Bill Werde, former editorial director of *Billboard*.

Despite her tremendous fame and success, Beyoncé has managed to remain humble and true to her roots. As one interviewer wrote, "She's too modest, sweet, and conscientious to come off like a diva."[53] Her choreographer, Frank Gatson Jr., has said that because Beyoncé is so pretty, some assume she is difficult, rude, or high maintenance. "But I've never seen someone so sweet," he said. "It trips me out. Knowing she wants to go off on somebody because somebody's [made her upset], she catches herself. She

the most exciting moments in my life. So I would like for Taylor to come out and have her moment."[2] Beyoncé gave Swift the stage, forfeiting her own chance to make an acceptance speech so that Swift could complete hers.

1. 2009 MTV Video Music Awards, MTV, September 13, 2009.

2. 2009 MTV Video Music Awards, MTV.

Beyoncé generously gave the microphone to Taylor Swift to let her finish her speech that Kanye West had interrupted earlier in the night.

knows that humility is important. I think it's her upbringing in church."[54] Indeed, Beyoncé has always been outspoken about her religious beliefs and frequently mentions her faith during interviews. She has also written about it in her autobiography, stating, "I know that God is a part of all of our lives. He lives in all of us."[55]

While Beyoncé is an exceptional talent, she also remains humble despite all the fame and recognition she receives. She knows how fleeting fame can be, accepts it, and focuses on staying grounded and thankful for every opportunity she has been given so far in life. "You can't get a big head, because it will be taken away from you in a second," she said. "A lot of artists don't understand that. They think that if they get a record, they'll be here forever."[56] Beyoncé strives to keep challenging herself and surprising her fans with each new album she releases and with every new project she signs on to do. It is her dedication to elevating her artistry, her natural talent, and her hard work that have placed her in the spotlight and will assure her legacy lives on for years to come.

Chapter **Five**

Building on Her Success

As Beyoncé continued to elevate her status as a monumental artist, she and JAY-Z decided to take the next step in their personal life together. For her performance of "Love on Top" at the 2011 MTV Video Music Awards, Beyoncé took the stage wearing a shimmering purple blazer. At the end of her performance, she dropped the microphone and ripped open her blazer to reveal a baby bump. The camera cut to a proud looking JAY-Z, who was being congratulated by his friend, rapper Kanye West.

Blue Ivy

After Beyoncé and JAY-Z announced her pregnancy, JAY-Z left for his *Watch the Throne* tour. During the middle of the tour, on January 7, 2012, Beyoncé gave birth to their first daughter—Blue Ivy Carter. Several people have speculated the significance of the child's name. For example, some point to the JAY-Z lyrics: "My favorite hue is Jay-Z blue,"[57] which appear in his rap verse in the Young Jeezy song "Go Crazy." He has also released multiple *Blueprint* albums throughout his career. Beyoncé's favorite number is four, which translates to "IV" in Roman numerals and is pronounced as "Ivy." She hinted at a possible source of inspiration for their daughter's name by posting an excerpt from a

JAY-Z and Blue Ivy presented Beyoncé with the Michael Jackson Video Vanguard Award at the 2014 MTV Video Music Awards.

2005 Rebecca Solnit novel called *A Field Guide to Getting Lost* on Tumblr in June 2012:

The world is blue at its edges and in its depths. This blue is the light that got lost. Light at the blue end of the spectrum does not travel the whole distance from the sun to us. It disperses among the molecules of the air, it scatters in the water. Water is colorless, shallow water appears to be the color of whatever lies underneath it, but deep water is full of this scattered light, the purer the water the deeper the blue. The sky is blue for the same reason, but the blue at the horizon, the blue of the land that seems to be dissolving into the sky, is a deeper, dreamier, melancholy blue, the blue at the farthest reaches of the places where you see for miles, the blue of distance. This light does not touch us, does not travel the whole distance, the light that gets lost, gives us the beauty of the world, so much of which is in the color blue.[58]

Just like her parents, Blue Ivy has made a name for herself as a performer, as she's been featured in a number of Beyoncé and JAY-Z songs. She was first featured in JAY-Z's track "Glory," which he dedicated to Blue Ivy and released on January 9, 2012. At only two days old, she is heard crying on the track, which details Beyoncé and JAY-Z's pregnancy struggles, including a miscarriage (the loss of a child before birth) Beyoncé suffered before becoming pregnant with their first child. At two years old, Blue Ivy also appeared on Beyoncé's track "Blue" from her self-titled 2013 album. She is also featured in the music video for the song, which was filmed in Rio de Janeiro, Brazil. Blue Ivy later made a cameo in Beyoncé's "Formation" music video. On JAY-Z's album *4:44*, which was released on July 6, 2017, Blue Ivy is featured on one of the three bonus tracks titled "Blue's Freestyle/We Family." She is heard freestyling on the track with lines such as, "Never seen a ceiling in my whole life."[59] On J Balvin and Willy William's remix of "Mi Gente," which features Beyoncé, Blue Ivy also makes a vocal cameo. The single's proceeds went to disaster victims in Mexico, Puerto Rico, and other Caribbean islands affected by Hurricanes Harvey, Irma, and Maria in 2017. Blue Ivy is also heard talking about her siblings on the end of Beyoncé and JAY-Z's track "Boss" from their joint album *Everything Is Love*, saying, "Shout-out to Rumi and Sir. Love, Blue."[60]

Super Bowl Halftime Show

In October 2012, it was announced that Beyoncé would be the halftime show performer at Super Bowl XLVII. On February 3, 2013, Beyoncé took the stage at the Mercedes-Benz Superdome in New Orleans and opened her set with "Love on Top." Next, she transitioned into "Crazy in Love" and "End of Time" and was joined by her backup dancers. Her next song involved a screen popping up from behind her, as she danced beside multiplied projections of herself and performed her song "Baby Boy." After this was a surprise reunion of Destiny's Child, as Beyoncé's former bandmates Rowland and Williams joined her to sing "Bootylicious" and "Independent Women Part 1" as fire surrounded them. They also joined her on her own song "Single Ladies

(Put a Ring on It)" before they left the stage. She closed out the night surrounded by blue lights as she sang her powerful ballad "Halo."

Her Super Bowl performance received much praise, as one reviewer for the *New York Times* said, "She balanced explosions and humanity, imperiousness with warmth, an arena-ready sense of scale with a microscopic approach to the details of her vocals. Amid all the loudness were small things to indicate Beyoncé was answering her skeptics, quietly but effectively."[61]

Destiny's Child surprised the audience when they reunited during Beyoncé's Super Bowl halftime show in 2013.

Life Is But a Dream

Following her Super Bowl performance, Beyoncé won the Grammy for Best Traditional R&B Vocal Performance for "Love on Top." She also released a documentary about her life, *Life Is But a Dream*, on HBO. Beyoncé served as executive producer, co-director, co-writer, and the main subject of the film. The film begins with videos from her childhood in the suburbs of Houston. Her father is behind the camera, heard constantly praising Beyoncé. Then, the film focuses on Beyoncé's decision to no longer have her father manage her, which happened in 2011. She spoke on how this choice affected her:

> *I'm feeling very empty because of the relationship with my dad. I'm so fragile at this point and I feel like my soul has been tarnished … I think one of the biggest reasons I decided it was time for me to manage myself was because at some point you need your support system. You need your family. When you're trying to have an everyday conversation with your parents, you have to talk about scheduling, you have to talk about your album, performing and touring. It's just too stressful and it really affects your relationship. I needed boundaries and I think my dad needed boundaries.*[62]

Another sorrowful moment in the film is when she talks about her first pregnancy, which ended in a miscarriage. She spoke about how she heard the heartbeat early on and later, when she went in for another check-up, they told her there was no longer a heartbeat. After this, she wrote what she calls the "saddest song"[63] she has ever written and, she said, it was the best form of therapy for her since it was the saddest thing she has ever been through. The film also includes behind-the-scenes footage of her life in the studio, moments with JAY-Z, her pregnancy with Blue Ivy, rehearsals, and life on tour.

Residency and Self-Titled Surprise Album

Only four months after giving birth to Blue Ivy, Beyoncé held a three-night residency, Revel Presents: Beyoncé Live, at the former Revel Casino Hotel Atlantic City (which has now been renamed the Ocean Resort Casino) in Atlantic City, New Jersey. After the residency, she spent most of the summer with her family in the Hamptons, New York. There, she spent quality time with her daughter and started working on material for her new album, which would eventually become her self-titled, fifth studio album, *Beyoncé*. The album was released as a surprise, without any prior promotion or announcement, exclusively on iTunes and was first available in the early morning hours of December 13, 2013. This time around, Beyoncé wanted to take a different approach to releasing her music by not letting anyone else decide when her new album would come out. With all 14 tracks, she also released accompanying short films, making it a visual album for her fans. Beyoncé explained her unique vision:

> I see music. It's more than just what I hear. When I'm connected to something, I immediately see a visual or a series of images that are tied to a feeling or an emotion, a memory from my childhood, thoughts about life, my dreams or my fantasies. And they're all connected to the music.[64]

The album debuted at the top of the Billboard 200, which gave Beyoncé her fifth consecutive number 1 album. As far as sales go, the album sold more than 1 million records in just over 6 days. Guest artists on the album include Drake on "Mine," Frank Ocean on "Superpower," JAY-Z on "Drunk in Love," and Blue Ivy on "Blue." The themes vary from song to song on this album: body image on "Pretty Hurts," relationship issues on "Jealous," loss on "Heaven," love and motherhood on "Blue," and feminism on "Flawless," featuring words from the Nigerian writer Chimamanda Ngozi Adichie. In her own life, Beyoncé proved that she could be a wife, mother, and an international pop star. However, she also wants young girls to know they do not have to be someone's wife and should embrace their independence.

Performing Together

While she worked on material for her fifth album, Beyoncé also kicked off her fifth concert tour, the Mrs. Carter Show World Tour, which ran from April 15, 2013, to March 27, 2014, and included European, North American, Latin American, and Oceania dates. The title of the tour refers to her marriage to JAY-Z, who made numerous guest performance appearances

Forbes List

To say that the Knowles-Carters are fabulously wealthy seems like an understatement. According to *Forbes* magazine, in 2007 alone, the year before they married, Beyoncé earned $27 million and JAY-Z $83 million. Ten years later, in 2017, the pair topped *Forbes*'s Highest-Paid Celebrity Couples list, earning a combined $147 million thanks to live shows, endorsement deals, and revenue from their own companies. The tables turned this year, as Beyoncé earned more than JAY-Z; she brought in $105 million and JAY-Z $42 million. Beyoncé also topped *Forbes*'s Highest-Paid Women in Music list in 2017.

In 2018, the couple officially surpassed the billionaire mark. In total, Beyoncé has brought in $322 million to JAY-Z's $900 million, which put them at an estimated $1.255 billion. Most of Beyoncé's earnings come from record and tour sales, while JAY-Z makes most of his money from his own companies. After JAY-Z purchased TIDAL in 2015, both artists released their albums, including *Lemonade*, *4:44*, and their joint album *Everything Is Love*, exclusively on the music-streaming site and made impressive sums. Beyoncé also made *Forbes*'s America's Richest Self-Made Women list, landing at 53 behind Oprah Winfrey and Kylie Jenner.

during the tour. For the 2013 shows, Beyoncé performed songs from her first four albums, and in 2014, she started to incorporate songs from her self-titled fifth album. The tour received positive reception, as one reviewer called the show a "musical and visual extravaganza," serving as an event that saw "the multi-talented artist's intent to join the rarefied ranks of ultimate entertainer."[65]

Beyoncé and her backup dancers are shown here performing during her Mrs. Carter Show World Tour.

Beyoncé and JAY-Z also joined each other again for the opening of the 2014 Grammy Awards in January. The couple performed with each other during Beyoncé's "Drunk in Love." Beyoncé began the performance sitting in a chair with her back to the audience as lights flashed and smoke filled the stage. Throughout the performance, she sang and danced on a small rotating stage, danced with JAY-Z during his rapping section in the song, and pumped up the crowd with her husband.

After performing with each other at all these events, Beyoncé and JAY-Z decided to head out on an official joint tour. The couple released a trailer, "Run," in May 2014 to promote the forthcoming tour, which had them portraying outlaw, Bonnie and Clyde–type characters. Several actors, such as Blake Lively, Rashida Jones, Don Cheadle, Jake Gyllenhaal, and Sean Penn were featured in the trailer. At the end of the trailer, the words "Coming Never" popped up on the screen. During the tour, the couple performed their shared songs such as "03 Bonnie & Clyde," "Upgrade U," and "Crazy in Love" from their early careers. JAY-Z also performed songs from his 12th studio album, *Magna Carta Holy Grail*, while Beyoncé performed songs from her self-titled album. The On the Run Tour ran from June 25, 2014, to September 13, 2014, with most of the shows taking place in the United States and Canada, and two of them taking place in France.

Elevator Incident

Even though Beyoncé and JAY-Z's relationship may have seemed ideal because of how supportive they appeared to be of each other, this was not always the case. On May 5, 2014, Beyoncé found herself in the middle of a family altercation after the Met Gala. After attending the event, she and her husband headed to the Standard Hotel in New York City for a Met Gala after-party with her sister, Solange. While riding the elevator, Solange attacked JAY-Z, hitting and kicking him before being restrained by a security guard. At one point, Beyoncé intervened, trying to diffuse the situation. Unfortunately for all parties involved, the incident was caught on tape due to a video camera in the elevator. The surveillance footage of the attack was leaked by a hotel employee, who was later fired by the hotel for his actions, to

Beyoncé and Solange are very protective of one another.

the celebrity news website TMZ, which posted it for the public to see. A few days later, the three recording artists released a joint statement:

> As a result of the public release of the elevator security footage from Monday, May 5th, there has been a great deal of speculation about what triggered the unfortunate incident. But the most important thing is that our family has worked through it …
>
> Jay and Solange each assume their share of responsibility for what has occurred. They both acknowledge their role in this private matter that has played out in the public. They both have apologized to each other and we have moved forward as a united family.
>
> The reports of Solange being intoxicated or displaying erratic behavior throughout that evening are simply false … At the end of the day families have problems and we're no different. We love each other and above all we are family. We've put this behind us and hope everyone else will do the same.[66]

Several speculations of what caused the incident came out, from cheating to break-up rumors for the married couple. However, an official reason for the occurrence has never been addressed. Following the altercation, all three recording artists cleverly mentioned or alluded to the incident on their subsequent albums: Beyoncé's *Lemonade*, JAY-Z's *4:44*, and Solange's *A Seat at the Table*. The hype built up around both Beyoncé's and JAY-Z's albums after the incident was massive as everyone was wondering what really happened between the couple despite their picture-perfect lifestyle.

Chapter **Six**

Limitless Aspirations

Beyoncé's wide-ranging accomplishments include sell-ing millions of albums, starring in several films, putting together successful concert tours, operating as an intelligent businesswoman, and being a dedicated mother and faithful wife. However, rumors were circulating that JAY-Z could not make the same claim about his faithfulness toward Beyoncé. As time passed, many different theories were unearthed about why the elevator moment happened. Instead of letting the drama of the event fill her with frustration, Beyoncé used this as material for her next two albums, which proved to be a smart choice, since the success of those albums resulted in her becoming the first artist ever to have six consecutive albums debut at number 1.

Feminism Discussion

As gossip swirled regarding Beyoncé and JAY-Z's relationship, Beyoncé stayed quiet about the incident for the most part, other than the joint statement she released with JAY-Z and Solange, until she released the remix of her song "Flawless" featuring rap-per Nicki Minaj in August 2014. A lyric about an elevator served as playful commentary on the scuffle. In addition, she talked about how she is not just someone's wife and how she has ownership over her music and career.

When performing the song in front of an audience, the word "feminist" flashed across a black screen in huge pink letters with the following definition: "A person who believes in the social, political, and economic equality of the sexes."[67] Beyoncé told *Elle* magazine, "I put the definition of feminist in my song and on my tour, not for propaganda or to proclaim to the world that I'm a feminist, but to give clarity to the true meaning. I'm not really sure people know or understand what a feminist is, but it's very simple. It's someone who believes in equal rights for men and women."[68]

This clarification of feminism, however, received mixed reviews. Adichie, whose words from her TED talk speech "We should all be feminists" appear in the song, claimed, "[Beyoncé's] type of feminism is not mine, as it is the kind that, at the same time, gives quite a lot of space to the necessity of men. I think men are lovely, but I don't think that women should relate everything they do to men."[69] Singer Annie Lennox also called out Beyoncé, calling this display of feminism "feminist lite":

It's tokenistic to me. I mean, I think she's a phenomenal artist – I just love her performances – but I'd like to sit down (with her). … I see a lot of it as them taking the word hostage and using it to promote themselves, but I don't think they necessarily represent wholeheartedly the depths of feminism.[70]

As far as the song goes, it was named one of *TIME*'s Top Ten Songs of 2014 as part of its year-end series, and *Entertainment Weekly* placed the song at number 2 on its best songs of 2014 list.

Black Lives Matter

In the past, Beyoncé had been criticized for failing to address the topic of racial inequality in her music. However, after the deaths of unarmed black men Michael Brown and Eric Garner in 2014, Beyoncé began speaking out against police brutality and in favor of the Black Lives Matter movement. This movement was created in 2013 after 17-year-old Trayvon Martin was fatally shot by a Florida neighborhood watch captain, George Zimmerman, in February 2012. Black Lives Matter aims to expose incidences of police brutality, to protest against racism, and to liberate those who have been marginalized because of the color of their skin.

As part of her dedication toward supporting black civil rights, Beyoncé performed as part of a tribute to the movie *Selma* at the 2015 Grammys. She opened the night with her own rendition of the gospel song "Take My Hand, Precious Lord." Ledisi, who played the role of gospel singer Mahalia Jackson and sings the same song in the film, said she was disappointed Beyoncé was picked to perform the song instead of her, but ultimately, she was understanding about the decision. Beyoncé spoke about her father's connections to the civil rights movement: "My grandparents marched with Dr. King, and my father was part of the first generation of black men that attended an all white school. My father has grown up with a lot of trauma from those experiences. I feel like now I can sing for my father's pain."[71] Common and

Beyoncé performed "Take My Hand, Precious Lord" with a choir of backup singers at the 2015 Grammys.

John Legend also performed their song "Glory," the track they created for the film, for the special tribute.

With the release of her song and music video "Formation," Beyoncé joined in on the commentary surrounding racial issues. There are several references to black culture and former and current examples of racial inequality in the United States. The opening shot in the video is of Beyoncé crouching down on top of a New Orleans police car sinking in water. This image references the condition of New Orleans after Hurricane Katrina in 2005 and how rebuilding took longer than it should have in lower income areas, which had a predominately black population. Near the end of the music video for the song, a young black boy is seen dancing in front of a line of police officers and puts his hands up. The police officers respond by putting their hands up as well. This image is followed by the message "Stop Shooting Us" written across a wall, which is in reference to the fight against police brutality and for justice for the many recent deaths of unarmed black men.

On February 7, 2016, Beyoncé continued with her theme of black empowerment during her guest performance at the Super Bowl 50 halftime show, which was headlined by British rock group Coldplay and also featured Bruno Mars. She performed "Formation" while flanked on the football field by her crew of dancers, who were all dressed as a tribute to the Black Panther Party, a political party that worked to protect the rights of black people. After singing the song, she joined Mars on the main stage for a dance-off. All three acts ended the performance by singing "Uptown Funk," which is originally by Mark Ronson featuring Mars.

After her performance, she received mixed reactions from the media, with some people supporting her and some in disapproval of it. Former New York mayor Rudy Giuliani criticized Beyoncé for her support of Black Lives Matter in the halftime show: "This is football, not Hollywood, and I thought it was really outrageous that she used it as a platform to attack police officers who are the people who protect her and protect us, and keep us alive."[72] Black Lives Matter activist Erika Totten supported Beyoncé's message: "I think [the message] absolutely belongs in the Super Bowl. Our goal is to disrupt the status quo and bring the message wherever the message may not be heard."[73]

Beyoncé joined Chris Martin of Coldplay (center) and Bruno Mars (right) on stage at the Super Bowl 50 halftime show.

Lemonade

On April 16, 2016, Beyoncé released a cryptic trailer revealing a project titled *Lemonade*, which would air on HBO a week later as a 65-minute conceptual musical film. After the airing of the film, she also released her sixth album of the same name exclusively to TIDAL, which had no prior promotion. TIDAL described the album as a "conceptual project based on every woman's journey of self-knowledge and healing."[74]

The film corresponded to the album, as all 12 songs from the album are featured. The impressive cinematic quality of the film is thanks to several people, such as Kahlil Joseph, Melina Matsoukas, Dikayl Rimmasch, Mark Romanek, Todd Tourso, Jonas Åkerlund, and Beyoncé herself, all of whom assisted in directing the film, which is divided into 11 chapters: "Intuition," "Denial," "Anger," "Apathy," "Emptiness," "Accountability," "Reformation," "Forgiveness," "Resurrection," "Hope," and "Redemption."

Throughout the film, Beyoncé recites poetry and prose written by Somali-British poet Warsan Shire, including "The Unbearable Weight of Staying," "Dear Moon," "How to Wear Your Mother's Lipstick," "Nail Technician as Palm Reader," and "For Women Who Are Difficult to Love." She also uses a sample from the Malcolm X speech "Who Taught You to Hate Yourself" on the song "Don't Hurt Yourself." Some of the guest appearances in the film include tennis player Serena Williams, actresses Quvenzhané Wallis and Amandla Stenberg, Nigerian artist Laolu Senbanjo, French musical duo Ibeyi, singers Chloe x Halle, and actress and singer Zendaya. One emotional part of the film features the mothers of Trayvon Martin, Michael Brown, and Eric Garner holding photos up of their deceased sons during the song "Forward."

Guest artists featured on the album include Jack White on "Don't Hurt Yourself," James Blake on "Forward," the Weeknd on "6 Inch," and Kendrick Lamar on "Freedom." Beyoncé has cited her grandmother Agnéz Deréon and JAY-Z's grandmother Hattie White as inspirations for the album title. A clip of White speaking to the crowd at her 90th birthday in April 2015 is heard at the end of the song "Freedom": "I had my ups and downs, but I always find the inner strength to pull myself up. I was served lemons, but I made lemonade."[75]

Numerous themes appear throughout *Lemonade*, such as anger, betrayal, black identity, sisterhood, Christian faith, and marital infidelity, the last of which sparked rumors of JAY-Z and Beyoncé's marriage potentially falling apart. One particular line in Beyoncé's song "Sorry," which struck up controversy among fans was, "He better call Becky with the good hair."[76] This line seems to point to a specific person, which many fans claim as someone who JAY-Z may have had romantic relations with during his marriage. However, Diana Gordon, one of the main songwriters for the track, was surprised at how much reaction and speculation came from fans regarding the song lyric: "I laughed [at the reaction], like this is so silly. Where are we living? I was like, 'What day in age from that lyric do you get all of this information?' Is it really telling you all that much, accusing people?"[77] Another song that references marital infidelity is "Hold Up." In the video for the song, Beyoncé is heard asking, "Are you cheating on me?"[78] while submerged in water.

Lemonade debuted at number 1 on the Billboard 200 chart, and it was the best-selling album of 2016, with 2.5 million copies shipped globally. Beyoncé was nominated for nine awards at the 2017 Grammys; she ended up winning Best Urban Contemporary Album for *Lemonade* and Best Music Video for "Formation." *Lemonade* also won a Peabody Award in Entertainment, as the board of jurors said,

> Lemonade *draws from the prolific literary, musical, cinematic, and aesthetic sensibilities of black cultural producers to create a rich tapestry of poetic innovation. The audacity of its reach and fierceness of its vision challenges our cultural imagination, while crafting a stunning and sublime masterpiece about the lives of women of color and the bonds of friendship seldom seen or heard in American popular culture.*[79]

Formation World Tour

Beyoncé kicked off her Formation World Tour on April 27, 2016, which ran until October 7 of that year, playing dates in North America and Europe. Some of the special features of the show included a 60-foot (18.3 m) tall rotating cube and a stage area that filled up with 2,000 gallons (7,570 L) of water for Beyoncé and her dancers to perform in. A *Rolling Stone* reviewer wrote that the show was "a prime example of entertainment and a vision of an artist at her apex" and "a visual feast as well as an emotional tour de force, packed with fireworks, confetti, rearranging stage designs and aerial dancers."[80]

In addition to her tour, Beyoncé opened the 2016 BET Awards with a performance of "Freedom" with Lamar in June.

In August, she also performed a 16-minute medley of the songs "Pray You Catch Me," "Hold Up," "Sorry," "Don't Hurt Yourself," and "Formation" at the MTV Video Music Awards. *Rolling Stone's* Rob Sheffield wrote that it was "one of the most blood-chillingly great live performances in award-show history."[81] She also went home with the Video Music Award for Video of the Year for "Formation" and Best Female Video for "Hold Up."

Beyoncé received a standing ovation after her performance at the 2016 MTV Video Music Awards.

Birth of Twins

At the beginning of 2017, Beyoncé revealed she was pregnant with twins. She posted a photo to her official Instagram page on February 1 of her kneeling in front of a large bouquet of flowers while wearing a green veil and holding her stomach. The photo's caption read, "We would like to share our love and happiness. We have been blessed two times over. We are incredibly grateful that our family will be growing by two, and we thank you for your well wishes."[82] This photo became the most-liked photo on Instagram in 2017, as it generated 11.1 million likes in just hours.

On February 12, Beyoncé performed her songs "Love Drought" and "Sandcastles" while pregnant and wearing a golden gown and headdress at the 2017 Grammy Awards. During much of the performance, she was surrounded by various projections of three generations of her family, including her mother and Blue Ivy. At one point, she also sat in a chair, which mechanically dipped back as she sang and her dancers leaned toward her and danced among their own chairs.

On July 13, 2017, Beyoncé posted another photo, this time to celebrate her one-month-old twins, Rumi and Sir, who were born on June 13 at Ronald Reagan UCLA Medical Center in Los Angeles. In the photo, she is seen standing in front of a display of flowers while wearing a light blue veil and holding her newborn children.

Beyoncé performed at the 2017 Grammys while pregnant with twins.

Coachella

Beyoncé became the first black woman to headline the Coachella music festival in 2018. She performed two Saturdays in a row, with her first performance on April 14, which saw her break viewership records on YouTube with her 105-minute set, pulling in 458,000 simultaneous viewers globally, making it the most watched Coachella performance ever. *New York Times* reviewer Jon Caramanica wrote, "There's not likely to be a more meaningful, absorbing, forceful, and radical performance by an American musician this year, or any year soon, than Beyoncé's headlining set at [Coachella] Saturday night."[1]

During her set, she featured over 100 live dancers and a full HBCU (historically black colleges and universities) marching band. The singer also brought out special guests, such as JAY-Z for "Déjà vu," Solange for "Get Me Bodied," and Rowland and Williams for a Destiny's Child reunion performance, as they sang "Say My Name," "Soldier," and "Lose My Breath." She also incorporated songs by Master P, Crucial Conflict, Juvenile, C-Murder, and Fast Life Yungstaz. Beyoncé performed the following Saturday on April 21 as well, but only the first weekend's performance was taped and made available online.

In an interview with *Vogue*, Beyoncé spoke about what she wants to teach both her daughters and her son:

As the mother of two girls, it's important to me that they see themselves … as CEOs, as bosses, and that they know they can write the script for their own lives—that they can speak their minds and they have no ceiling. They don't have to be

After Beyoncé's one-of-a-kind performance at Coachella, several people nicknamed that year's festival Beychella.

1. Quoted in John Flynn and Natalie Somekh, "Beyoncé Reigns, Rock Dies: Coachella 2018 Festival Review," Consequenceofsound.net, April 16, 2018. consequenceofsound. net/2018/04/beyonce-reigns-rock-dies-coachella-2018-festival-review/.

a certain type or fit into a specific category. They don't have to be politically correct, as long as they're authentic, respectful, compassionate, and empathetic. They can explore any religion, fall in love with any race, and love who they want to love. I want the same things for my son. I want him to know that he can be strong and brave but that he can also be sensitive and kind. I want my son to have a high emotional

IQ where he is free to be caring, truthful, and honest. It's everything a woman wants in a man, and yet we don't teach it to our boys.[83]

Release of 4:44

Once Beyoncé released *Lemonade*, with its references to JAY-Z's cheating, the public was wondering if these claims were true or just another publicity stunt to increase album sales. They also were waiting to hear JAY-Z's side of the story. Luckily, on June 30, 2017, JAY-Z released his 13th album, *4:44*, which addressed the cheating rumors. Beyoncé is featured on the album's track "Family Feud."

Throughout the title track on *4:44*, JAY-Z hints at his cheating and seems to apologize to his wife for his behavior: "I apologize to all the women whom I/ Toyed with your emotions 'cause I was emotionless/ And I apologize 'cause at your best you are love/ And because I fall short of what I say I'm all about/ Your eyes leave with the soul that your body once housed."[84] In the last verse of the song, he also speaks about his children regarding his past mistakes: "And if my children knew/ I don't even know what I would do/ If they ain't look at me the same/ I would prob'ly die with all the shame."[85]

In an exclusive *New York Times* interview with Dean Baquet, JAY-Z revealed he was unfaithful to Beyoncé and talked about coming to terms with what he had done. He also spoke on the challenge of facing the problems in their relationship and how they resolved them: "The best place is right in the middle of the pain. And that's where we were sitting. And it was uncomfortable. And we had a lot of conversations. [I was] really proud of the music she made, and she was really proud of the art I released. And, you know, at the end of the day we really have a healthy respect for one another's craft. I think she's amazing."[86]

Originally, these two albums were meant to become a joint album. However, Beyoncé's music was further along than JAY-Z's, so she released her album first and JAY-Z's followed. Through helping each other with their albums, the pair made music together "almost like a therapy session," JAY-Z said. "I was right there the entire time."[87]

Making Music Together

Beyoncé and JAY-Z announced their On the Run II Tour on March 12, 2018. The tour had two legs, the first in Europe and the second in North America, running from June 6 to October 4. After their London show on June 16, the couple revealed their first joint album as the Carters titled *Everything Is Love*, made available exclusively first on TIDAL and later to other retailers. After the release, they started incorporating music from the album into their set list. The album landed at number 2 on the Billboard 200 chart.

The themes covered on the album included the couple's relationship and romance, fame and media worship, black pride, and also how they dealt with issues in their relationship. A review of the album stated that it is "like the fifth act of a hip-hop and R&B Shakespearean comedy, *Everything Is Love* finds our lovers reunited, their misunderstandings resolved, their vows

Beyoncé and JAY-Z are shown here sharing a kiss while on stage during their On the Run II Tour.

Chloe x Halle

As Beyoncé has had numerous role models in her life who have inspired her to never back down and to strive to be the best, she also hopes to be that inspiration for many others: "Imagine if someone hadn't given a chance to the brilliant women who came before me: Josephine Baker, Nina Simone, Eartha Kitt, Aretha Franklin, Tina Turner, Diana Ross, Whitney Houston, and the list goes on. They opened the doors for me, and I pray that I'm doing all I can to open doors for the next generation of talents."[1]

Chloe x Halle, an R&B duo that caught the eye of Beyoncé, made up of sisters Chloe and Halle Bailey, were inspired by Beyoncé to become singers. Beyoncé first discovered them on YouTube after they had posted a video of their own cover of her song "Pretty Hurts." In 2013, they were signed to Beyoncé's Parkwood Entertainment company, which was started in 2008. The sisters released their first album, *The Kids Are Alright*, on March 23, 2018, and they star on the series *Grown-ish*, which is a spin-off of the ABC series *Black-ish*. Halle commented on the helpful advice Beyoncé gave to them: "Being in the midst of having such a beautiful mentor like her, we were allowed to explore with our creativity, and we're so thankful to her for providing her platform and always reminding us that you don't have to dumb down your art for the world — you can keep creating new, innovative things and let the world catch up to you."[2]

1. Beyoncé, "Beyoncé in Her Own Words: Her Life, Her Body, Her Heritage," *Vogue*, August 6, 2018. www.vogue.com/article/beyonce-september-issue-2018.

2. Quoted in Jeff Nelson, "Chloe x Halle Talk Advice from Beyoncé—and Why 'She Is Just the Best Human Being Ever,'" *People*, March 23, 2018. people.com/music/chloe-x-halle-beyonce-mentor-advice-dont-get-starstruck-anymore/.

renewed, and their family looking ahead to decades of more peaceful prosperity."[88]

On the album's track "LOVEHAPPY," Beyoncé said, "You [screwed] up the first stone, we had to get remarried,"[89] referencing JAY-Z's infidelity, but also the renewal of their vows. The couple appeared in footage played during their On the Run II concerts while they sang JAY-Z's song "Young Forever" together. At one point, the footage features both of them wearing white wedding attire and embracing each other while renewing their vows, and it also shows them with their children.

The Future of a Queen

Even though Beyoncé has experienced ups and downs in her life and career, she always trudges ahead to create a brighter future for herself. She has successfully achieved goals beyond even what she thought was possible.

After going through a tough time with her husband, they reconciled, coming to an agreement that their love and the love of their family is most important to them. While she may be a huge pop superstar, Beyoncé has had to overcome family issues and life struggles similar to what everyday people have to go through. She spoke about her life-changing experiences with *Vogue*: "I have experienced betrayals and heartbreaks in many forms. I have had disappointments in business partnerships as well as personal ones, and they all left me feeling neglected, lost, and vulnerable. Through it all I have learned to laugh and cry and grow."[90]

Despite the hardships, she has come out on the other side a stronger, more confident, and capable person and artist. She is recognized by many of her fans as a queen, and rightfully so, as she is able to continue to thrive and move forward in life and in music with immense talent, style, and grace. The future is wide open for Beyoncé, and her loyal and supportive fans are always waiting in anticipation for whatever grand idea "Queen Bey" chooses to bring to life next.

Notes

Introduction: The Fate of a True Superstar

1. Quoted in "Beyonce Reveals Song for Obamas' First Dance at Inaugural Ball," MTV News, January 16, 2009. www.mtv.com/news/articles/1602946/beyonce-reveals-song-obamas-first-dance.jhtml.

2. Beyoncé Knowles, Kelly Rowland, and Michelle Williams, with James Patrick Herman, *Soul Survivors: The Official Biography of Destiny's Child*. New York, NY: HarperCollins, 2002, p. 19.

3. Quoted in Dimitri Ehrlich, "Beyoncé: Diamond Life (2003 Cover Story & Gallery)," *Complex*, June 3, 2011. www.complex.com/music/2011/06/beyonce-2003-cover-story-gallery.

Chapter One: A Star in the Making

4. Beyoncé Knowles, "Eat, Play, Love," *Essence*, July 2011. www.essence.com/news/beyonce-knowles-nyabj-award-essence-article-eat-play-love/.

5. Knowles, "Eat, Play, Love."

6. Quoted in Simon Garfield, "Uh-Oh! Uh-Oh! Uh-Oh!," *The Guardian*, December 14, 2003. www.guardian.co.uk/music/2003/dec/14/popandrock1.

7. Quoted in James Patrick Herman, "Becoming Beyonce: 20 Things You Don't Know About the Singer's Journey to Superstardom," ETonline.com, February 10, 2017. www.etonline.com/features/210034_beyonce_and_her_journey_to_superstardom.

8. Quoted in Mimi Valdés, "The Metamorphosis," *Vibe*, June 28, 2011. www.vibe.com/2011/06/beyonce-metamorphosis-october-2002-pg2/.

9. Quoted in Valdés, "The Metamorphosis."

10. Quoted in J. Randy Taraborrelli, *Becoming Beyonce: The Untold Story*. London, UK: Pan Books, 2016. E-book.

11. Knowles, Rowland, and Williams, *Soul Survivors*, p. 53.

Chapter Two: Finding Success with Destiny's Child

12. Knowles, Rowland, and Williams, *Soul Survivors*, p. 81.

13. Knowles, Rowland, and Williams, *Soul Survivors*, p. 87.

14. Quoted in Ehrlich, "Beyoncé: Diamond Life."

15. Knowles, Rowland, and Williams, *Soul Survivors*, p. 62.

16. Knowles, Rowland, and Williams, *Soul Survivors*, p. 99.

17. Knowles, Rowland, and Williams, *Soul Survivors*, p. 99.

18. Quoted in Jevaillier Jefferson, "The Big Break That Launched My Career," *Black Collegian Online*. www.black-collegian.com/career/bigbreak2003-1st.shtml.

Chapter Three: Becoming a Solo Artist

19. Knowles, Rowland, and Williams, *Soul Survivors*, p. 216.

20. Quoted in Valdés, "The Metamorphosis."

21. Steven Oxman, "Carmen: A Hip Hopera," *Variety*, May 2, 2001. variety.com/2001/tv/reviews/carmen-a-hip-hopera-1200468590/.

22. Knowles, Rowland, and Williams, *Soul Survivors*, p. 254.

23. Knowles, Rowland, and Williams, *Soul Survivors*, p. 255.

24. Knowles, Rowland, and Williams, *Soul Survivors*, p. 255.

25. Roger Ebert, "Austin Powers in Goldmember," RogerEbert.com, July 26, 2002. rogerebert.suntimes.com/apps/pbcs.dll/article?AID=/20020726/REVIEWS/207260301/1023.

26. Quoted in Karen Bliss, "Beyonce Gets Dangerous," *Rolling Stone*, November 12, 2002. www.rollingstone.com/music/news/beyonce-gets-dangerous-20021112.

27. Beyoncé Knowles, *46th Grammy Awards*, CBS, February 8, 2004.

28. Quoted in MTV Networks, "Beyoncé: Genuinely in Love," MTV.com, June 27, 2003. www.mtv.com/bands/b/beyonce/news_feature_062703/index2.jhtml.

29. Quoted in Garfield, "Uh-Oh! Uh-Oh! Uh-Oh!"

30. Tom Sinclair, "Music Review: *Destiny Fulfilled* (2004)," *Entertainment Weekly*, November 26, 2004. www.ew.com/ew/article/0,,784896,00.html.

31. Quoted in Denise Sheppard, "Destiny's Child Take a Bow," *Rolling Stone*, September 12, 2005. www.rollingstone.com/music/news/destinys-child-take-a-bow-20050912.

Chapter Four: Owning Her Star Power

32. Quoted in Shawn Adler, "Beyonce, Etta James and 'Cadillac Records' Stars Come Out for Movie's Premiere," MTV News, November 25, 2008. www.mtv.com/news/1600243/beyonce-etta-james-and-cadillac-records-stars-come-out-for-movies-premiere/.

33. Sarah Rodman, "Beyoncé Shows Rage and Range on New Release," *Boston Globe*, September 4, 2006. archive.boston.com/news/globe/living/articles/2006/09/04/beyonce_shows_rage_and_range_on_new_release/.

34. Anthony Venutolo, "Beyonce Bedazzles," *The Star-Ledger*, August 6, 2007. blog.nj.com/ledgerentertainment/2007/08/beyonce_bedazzles.html.

35. James Reed, "Beyoncé Sets Her Softer Side Free in Low-Key '4,'" *Boston Globe*, June 26, 2011. archive.boston.com/ae/music/cd_reviews/articles/2011/06/26/cd_review_beyonc_shows_a_softer_side_on_4/.

36. Quoted in Associated Press, "Beyonce Transforms into 'Sasha' Onstage," *China Daily*, December 16, 2006. www.chinadaily.com.cn/entertainment/2006-12/16/content_760585.htm.

37. Kyle Anderson, "Beyoncé's Alter-Ego Tops the Charts: Wake-Up Video," MTV Newsroom, December 6, 2010. newsroom.mtv.com/2010/12/06/beyonce-i-am-sasha-fierce-number-one.

38. Christian Hoard, "Beyoncé: *I Am… Sasha Fierce*," *Rolling Stone*, November 27, 2008. www.rollingstone.com/music/albumreviews/i-am-sasha-fierce-20081127.

39. Leah Greenblatt, "Music Review: *I Am … Sasha Fierce* (2008)," *Entertainment Weekly*, November 5, 2008. www.ew.com/ew/article/0,,20237810,00.html.

40. Quoted in Mariel Concepcion, "Beyoncé Is *Billboard*'s Woman of the Year," *Billboard*, August 25, 2009. www.billboard.com/articles/news/267596/beyonce-is-billboards-woman-of-the-year.

41. Quoted in Mariel Concepcion,"Beyoncé Accepts *Billboard*'s Woman of the Year Award, Lady Gaga Is Rising Star," *Billboard*,

October 2, 2009. www.billboard.com/articles/news/267205/beyonce-accepts-billboards-woman-of-the-year-award-lady-gaga-is-rising-star.

42. Quoted in NME, "Beyonce: 'I Took a Break From Music to Protect My Mental Health,'" *NME*, July 30, 2011. www.nme.com/news/music/beyonce-306-1277897.

43. Quoted in Sara McGinnis, "Beyonce's Year Off From Music: 'Eat, Play, Love,'" SheKnows.com, June 3, 2011. www.sheknows.com/entertainment/articles/832753/beyonces-year-off-from-musice-eat-play-love.

44. Matthew Horton, "Beyoncé 4 Review," BBC Music, June 22, 2011. www.bbc.co.uk/music/reviews/zw4z.

45. Reed, "Beyoncé Sets Her Softer Side Free in Low-Key '4.'"

46. Quoted in Valdés, "The Metamorphosis," p. 118.

47. Jon Caramanica, "Closer to Her Fans and Further Away from Her Past," *New York Times*, August 15, 2011. www.nytimes.com/2011/08/16/arts/music/beyonce-showcases-4-at-roseland-ballroom-review.html?_r=2&emc=eta1.

48. Quoted in Lisa Robinson, "Above and Beyoncé," *Vanity Fair*, November 2005. www.vanityfair.com/culture/2005/11/beyonce-knowles-profile-music-career.

49. Caramanica, "Closer to Her Fans and Further Away from Her Past."

50. Quoted in Valdés, "The Metamorphosis," p. 117.

51. Robinson, "Above and Beyoncé," p. 336.

52. Quoted in Concepcion, "Beyonce Accepts *Billboard*'s Woman of the Year Award."

53. Ehrlich, "Beyoncé: Diamond Life."

54. Quoted in Touré, "Beyonce Talks Fame, Relationships, Starting a Family, Becoming Sasha Fierce," *Rolling Stone*, March 4, 2004. www.rollingstone.com/music/music-features/beyonce-talks-fame-relationships-starting-a-family-becoming-sasha-fierce-111695/.

55. Knowles, Rowland, and Williams, *Soul Survivors*, p. 75.

56. Quoted in Jancee Dunn, "Date with Destiny," *The Guardian*, June 9, 2001. www.guardian.co.uk/theobserver/2001/jun/10/life1.lifemagazine5.

Chapter Five: Building on Her Success

57. Quoted in Ariana Finlayson, "Beyonce Hints at What Inspired Blue Ivy's Name," *Us Weekly*, June 14, 2012. www.usmagazine.com/celebrity-moms/news/beyonce-hints-at-what-inspired-blue-ivys-name-2012146/.

58. Quoted in Finlayson, "What Inspired Blue Ivy's Name."

59. Quoted in Max Weinstein, "Blue Ivy Is Rapping on JAY-Z's '4:44' Bonus Track," XXLmag, July 6, 2017. www.xxlmag.com/news/2017/07/blue-ivy-rapping-jay-z-444-bonus-track/.

60. The Carters, "Boss," Parkwood. Originally released June 16, 2018.

61. Jon Caramanica, "Beyoncé Silences Doubters With Intensity at Halftime," *New York Times*, February 4, 2013. www.nytimes.com/2013/02/04/sports/football/beyonce-brings-intensity-to-halftime-show-and-silences-doubters.html.

62. Quoted in "Beyoncé – Life Is But a Dream (Full Documentary)," YouTube Video, 1:30:01, posted by Mist, December 2, 2014. www.youtube.com/watch?v=VJizQTAySGQ.

63. Quoted in "Beyoncé – Life Is But a Dream (Full Documentary)."

64. Quoted in Ella Alexander, "Beyoncé Makes Music History," *Vogue*, December 13, 2013. www.vogue.co.uk/gallery/beyonce-releases-surprise-fifth-album-on-itunes.

65. Gail Mitchell, "Beyoncé Shines on U.S. Tour Launch in L.A.: Live Review," *Billboard*, June 29, 2013. www.billboard.com/articles/news/1568692/beyonce-shines-on-us-tour-launch-in-la-live-review.

66. Quoted in Associated Press, "Beyoncé, Jay Z and Solange Break Silence About Video Drama," *People*, May 15, 2014. people.com/celebrity/beyonc-jay-z-and-solange-break-silence-about-video-drama/.

Chapter Six: Limitless Aspirations

67. "Beyoncé – Flawless (Remix) ft. Nicki Minaj," YouTube video, 5:13, posted by Beyoncé, October 6, 2014. www.youtube.com/watch?v=56qgO0C82vY.

68. Quoted in Olivia Blair, "Beyoncé Explains Why She Performed in Front of the Word 'Feminist,'" *Independent*,

April 5, 2016. www.independent.co.uk/news/people/beyonce-explains-performed-in-front-of-the-word-feminist-flawless-formation-a6970256.html.

69. Quoted in Lily Kuo, "Chimamanda Adichie Says Beyonce's Kind of Feminism Isn't Her Kind of Feminism," QZ.com, October 9, 2016. qz.com/africa/804863/chimamanda-adichie-says-beyonces-kind-of-feminism-isnt-her-kind-of-feminism/.

70. Quoted in Chris Azzopardi, "Q&A: Annie Lennox on Her Legacy, Why Beyonce Is 'Feminist Lite,'" PrideSource.com, September 25, 2014. pridesource.com/article/68228-2/.

71. Quoted in Mailonline Reporter, "Beyoncé Explains Her Selma Tribute at the Grammys ... But Fails to Mention Original Choice Ledisi Who Reveals 'Disappointment' After Being Bumped From the Show," *Daily Mail*, February 10, 2015. www.dailymail.co.uk/tvshowbiz/article-2948180/Beyonc-explains-Selma-tribute-Grammys-fails-mention-original-choice-Ledisi-reveals-disappointment-bumped-show.html.

72. Quoted in Deena Zaru, "Beyonce Gets Political at Super Bowl, Tribute to 'Black Lives Matter,'" CNN, August 16, 2017. www.cnn.com/2016/02/08/politics/beyonce-super-bowl-black-lives-matter/index.html.

73. Quoted in Zaru, "Beyonce Gets Political at Super Bowl, Tribute to 'Black Lives Matter.'"

74. Quoted in Brittany Spanos, "Beyonce Releases New Album 'Lemonade' on Tidal," *Rolling Stone*, April 24, 2016. www.rolling-stone.com/music/news/beyonce-releases-new-album-lemonade-on-tidal-20160423.

75. Quoted in Shannon Carlin, "Who Is Speaking About Lemonade on Beyoncé's 'Freedom'? Hattie White Has a Strong Connection to the Star," *Bustle*, April 26, 2016. www.bustle.com/articles/157022-who-is-speaking-about-lemonade-on-beyoncs-freedom-hattie-white-has-a-strong-connection-to-the.

76. Beyoncé, "Sorry," Parkwood. Originally released May 3, 2016.

77. Quoted in Jack Shepherd, "Beyoncé Writer Addresses 'Becky with the Good Hair' Lyric in 'Sorry,'" *Independent*, August 3, 2016. www.independent.co.uk/arts-entertainment/music/news/beyonce-diana-gordon-who-is-becky-meaning-sorry-a7169786.html.

78. Quoted in "Beyoncé – Hold Up (Video)," YouTube video, 5:16, posted by Beyoncé, September 4, 2016. www.youtube.com/watch?v=PeonBmeFR8o.

79. Margaret Blanchard, "Entertainment Winners Named for Peabody 30," Peabody Awards, April 20, 2017. www.peabodyawards.com/stories/story/entertainment-winners-named-for-peabody-30.

80. Kat Bein, "Beyonce Stuns with 'Lemonade' Debuts, Rousing Hits at Tour Kickoff," *Rolling Stone*, April 28, 2016. www.rollingstone.com/music/music-live-reviews/beyonce-stuns-with-lemonade-debuts-rousing-hits-at-tour-kickoff-36078/.

81. Rob Sheffield, "How Beyonce Demolished the 2016 Video Music Awards: Middle Fingers Up," *Rolling Stone*, August 29, 2016. www.rollingstone.com/music/music-features/how-beyonce-demolished-the-2016-video-music-awards-middle-fingers-up-248053/.

82. Quoted in Alexa Tietjen, "Beyoncé Reveals Her Second Pregnancy by Way of a Stylish Photo Shoot," WWD.com, February 1, 2017. wwd.com/eye/lifestyle/beyonce-announces-shes-pregnant-on-instagram-10773748/.

83. Beyoncé, "Beyoncé in Her Own Words: Her Life, Her Body, Her Heritage," *Vogue*, August 6, 2018. www.vogue.com/article/beyonce-september-issue-2018.

84. JAY-Z, "4:44," Roc Nation. Originally released July 11, 2017.

85. JAY-Z, "4:44."

86. Quoted in Dean Baquet, "JAY-Z & Dean Baquet," *New York Times*, November 29, 2017. www.nytimes.com/interactive/2017/11/29/t-magazine/jay-z-dean-baquet-interview.html.

87. Quoted in Baquet, "JAY-Z & Dean Baquet."

88. Carl Wilson, "Beyoncé and Jay-Z's New Album Is Like the Satisfying Finale of a Prestige Drama," Slate, June 18, 2018. slate.com/culture/2018/06/beyonce-and-jay-zs-new-album-as-the-carters-everything-is-love-reviewed.html.

89. The Carters, "Everything Is Love," Parkwood. Originally released June 16, 2018.

90. Beyoncé, "Beyoncé in Her Own Words."

Beyoncé Year by Year

1981

Beyoncé Giselle Knowles is born on September 4 in Houston, Texas.

1988

Beyoncé enters her first talent show and wins a local talent award.

1990

Beyoncé joins the singing and dancing group Girl's Tyme.

1993

Girl's Tyme competes on *Star Search* but loses; Mathew Knowles leaves his job to manage the group.

1995

Girl's Tyme signs recording contract with Silent Partner Productions and begins recording an album, but the label drops the group after several months.

1996

The group signs with Columbia Records and changes its name to Destiny's Child.

1997

Destiny's Child contributes the song "Killing Time" to the *Men in Black* soundtrack.

1998

Destiny's Child releases its debut album, *Destiny's Child*, which goes platinum.

1999

Destiny's Child releases its second album, *The Writing's on the Wall*; LeToya Luckett and LaTavia Roberson leave the group and file a lawsuit against Mathew Knowles.

2000

The Destiny's Child single "Independent Women Part 1" is included on the soundtrack of the movie *Charlie's Angels*.

2001

Survivor and its lead single "Survivor" are released; Beyoncé stars in the movie *Carmen: A Hip Hopera* and is named Songwriter of the Year by the American Society of Composers, Authors, and Publishers.

2002

Beyoncé plays Foxxy Cleopatra in the movie *Austin Powers in Goldmember* and is nominated for a Black Reel Award and an MTV Award for her performance; she signs an endorsement deal with PepsiCo, begins dating JAY-Z, and helps fund the Knowles-Rowland Center for Youth along with her family and Kelly Rowland.

2003

Beyoncé stars in *The Fighting Temptations*; releases her first solo album, *Dangerously in Love*, which wins a record-tying five Grammy Awards; and embarks on her first solo tour through Europe.

2004

Destiny's Child records its final album, *Destiny Fulfilled*; Beyoncé and Tina Knowles Lawson introduce their fashion line, House of Deréon.

2006

Beyoncé appears in *The Pink Panther* and *Dreamgirls* and releases her second solo album, *B'Day*.

2007

Beyoncé embarks on a world tour called the Beyoncé Experience; a DVD titled *The Beyoncé Experience: Live* is released.

2008

Beyoncé plays Etta James in *Cadillac Records* and is nominated for an NAACP Image Award for her performance; she also releases her third solo album, *I Am … Sasha Fierce*, which wins five Grammy Awards, and marries longtime boyfriend JAY-Z.

2009

Beyoncé is named *Billboard*'s Woman of the Year.

2011

Beyoncé begins managing her own career; releases her fourth album, *4*; directs the music video for her song "Party;" and announces her pregnancy at the MTV Video Music Awards.

2012

Beyoncé gives birth to daughter Blue Ivy Carter in January.

2013

Beyoncé performs at the halftime show at Super Bowl XLVII; releases the documentary *Life Is But a Dream*; kicks off the Mrs. Carter Show World Tour concert tour; releases her self-titled visual album; and voices Queen Tara in the animated movie *Epic*.

2014

Beyoncé performs with JAY-Z on their joint On the Run Tour and releases "Flawless" remix with Nicki Minaj.

2015

Beyoncé performs as part of a tribute to the movie *Selma* at the 2015 Grammys.

2016

Beyoncé performs "Formation" at the Super Bowl 50 halftime show; releases the concept album and film *Lemonade*; kicks off her Formation World Tour; and performs a 16-minute medley of songs from *Lemonade* at the MTV Video Music Awards.

2017

Beyoncé performs at the Grammys while pregnant; welcomes twins Rumi and Sir; and is featured on J Balvin and Willy William's remix of "Mi Gente."

2018

Beyoncé becomes the first black woman to headline Coachella; kicks off the On the Run II Tour with JAY-Z; and releases the joint album *Everything Is Love* with JAY-Z.

2019

Beyoncé voices Nala in *The Lion King*.

For More Information

Books

Easley, Daryl. *Crazy in Love: The Beyoncé Knowles Biography*. London, UK: Omnibus, 2011.
This book tells the story of Beyoncé Knowles-Carter's rise to success with Destiny's Child and her subsequent solo career, as well as of her personal life and marriage to JAY-Z.

Pointer, Anna. *Beyoncé: Running the World: The Biography*. London, UK: Coronet, 2015.
Beyoncé's personal and professional life are covered in this biography, which includes details about her marriage, being a mother to daughter Blue Ivy, her relationship with her father, and her life as one of the most famous female singers of her generation.

Shahidi, Afshin. *Prince: A Private View*. New York, NY: St. Martin's Press, 2017.
Beyoncé contributes a heartfelt foreword for this photo book about Prince, a major influence on her music and life, as well as her close friend.

Taraborrelli, J. Randy. *Becoming Beyoncé: The Untold Story*. London, UK: Sidgwick & Jackson, 2016.
This biography tells the story of Beyoncé's career in Girl's Tyme and Destiny's Child to her work today as a successful solo recording artist and businesswoman.

Trier-Bieniek, Adrienne. *The Beyoncé Effect: Essays on Sexuality, Race and Feminism*. Jefferson, NC: McFarland & Company, Inc., 2016.
This book of essays examines topics related to the music and life of Beyoncé. Some of the subjects covered include female empowerment, body image, racial equality, and gender studies.

Websites

Beyoncé on Facebook
(www.facebook.com/beyonce/)
Beyoncé's official Facebook page features exclusive photographs and videos from her performances, up-to-date tour dates, and information on new music releases.

Beyoncé on Instagram
(www.instagram.com/beyonce/?hl=en)
Beyoncé's official Instagram page shows her personal photographs and videos of her time rehearsing and performing on tour, downtime with her family and friends, and activism.

Beyoncé on Twitter
(twitter.com/beyonce)
Beyoncé's official Twitter page allows her to connect with fans and provide them with information on upcoming special events, album releases, and tour announcements.

Beyoncé's Official Website
(www.beyonce.com/)
The official website of Beyoncé Knowles-Carter contains the latest news and press releases, photos, videos, information on upcoming events and music releases, a biography, merchandise for purchase, and more.

Destiny's Child Official Website
(www.destinyschild.com)
This is the official website of Destiny's Child. It contains photos, videos, news, biographies, and more.

Index

Picture Credits

About the Author

Vanessa Oswald is an experienced freelance writer and editor who has written pieces for publications based in New York City and the Western New York area, which include *Resource* magazine, *The Public*, *Auxiliary* magazine, and *Niagara Gazette*. In her spare time, she enjoys dancing, traveling, reading, snowboarding, and attending live concerts.